UNSUSTAINABLE FEDERAL SPENDING AND THE DEBT LIMIT

HEARING

BEFORE THE

SUBCOMMITTEE ON OVERSIGHT AND INVESTIGATIONS

OF THE

COMMITTEE ON FINANCIAL SERVICES

U.S. HOUSE OF REPRESENTATIVES

ONE HUNDRED FOURTEENTH CONGRESS

SECOND SESSION

FEBRUARY 2, 2016

Printed for the use of the Committee on Financial Services

Serial No. 114–69

U.S. GOVERNMENT PUBLISHING OFFICE

23–564 PDF   WASHINGTON : 2017

For sale by the Superintendent of Documents, U.S. Government Publishing Office
Internet: bookstore.gpo.gov   Phone: toll free (866) 512–1800; DC area (202) 512–1800
Fax: (202) 512–2104   Mail: Stop IDCC, Washington, DC 20402–0001

CONTENTS

UNSUSTAINABLE FEDERAL SPENDING AND THE DEBT LIMIT

Tuesday, February 2, 2016

U.S. House of Representatives,
Subcommittee on Oversight
and Investigations,
Committee on Financial Services,
Washington, D.C.

The subcommittee met, pursuant to notice, at 2:05 p.m., in room 2128, Rayburn House Office Building, Hon. Sean P. Duffy [chairman of the subcommittee] presiding.

Members present: Representatives Duffy, Fitzpatrick, Mulvaney, Hultgren, Wagner, Tipton, Poliquin, Hill; Green, Delaney, Beatty, Heck, and Sinema.

Also present: Representative Schweikert.

Chairman DUFFY. The Subcommittee on Oversight and Investigations is called to order.

The subject of today's hearing, as evidenced by the rapidly changing graphic on the screens around us, is, "Unsustainable Federal Spending and the Debt Limit."

We have a series of votes coming up, so we will proceed with our first panel of witnesses. Welcome to the Honorable Tom McClintock, who represents the 4th Congressional District in California. Next, we have the Honorable Mark Pocan, who represents one of the great States, if not the greatest State, Wisconsin, from the 2nd Congressional District.

With that, Mr. McClintock, you are recognized for 5 minutes for your opening statement.

STATEMENT OF THE HONORABLE TOM MCCLINTOCK, A REPRESENTATIVE IN CONGRESS FROM THE STATE OF CALIFORNIA

Mr. MCCLINTOCK. Thank you, Mr. Chairman.

Our government's good credit is vital to everything that we do here. And there are two ways to wreck that credit: by borrowing too much; or by failing to pay it back on time and in full.

Congress alone has the constitutional power to tax, to borrow, and to spend. We regulate our borrowing through the debt limit. And when we need to increase it, we have a duty to review and revise the policies that are driving it.

The United States now staggers under $19 trillion of debt, nearly half of it run up in the last 8 years. The interest on that debt is the fastest-growing component of the Federal budget. Within 5 years, it will consume more than we now spend for our entire defense establishment. That is why we dare not increase the debt without also correcting what is causing it.

But that can often lead to temporary impasses. And when that happens, it is vital that credit markets maintain supreme confidence in the security of their loans, otherwise the interest rates that lenders charge us would quickly rise to account for the increased risk, and our precarious budget situation would rapidly spin out of control.

The organic law that established the Treasury Department in 1789 specifically says that it shall be the duty of the Secretary of the Treasury to digest and prepare plans for the improvement and management of the revenue and for the support of the public credit.

"Manage the revenue and support the public credit:" the GAO clearly spelled out what that means in answering the Senate Finance Committee in 1985: "Treasury is free to liquidate obligations in any order it finds will best serve the interests of the United States."

The Constitution commands that the public debt is not to be questioned, and this is the practical mechanism for it. Most State constitutions provide that first call on any revenues is to maintain and protect their sovereign credit.

Now, that brings us to the fine point of the matter. In recent years, the Treasury Department has denied that it has either the ability or the authority to do so. Well, we now know from documents that were recently uncovered by this committee that this was a deliberate and calculated lie told to increase political pressure on Congress. We also know the Treasury Department was actually preparing contingency plans to prioritize debt at the same time the Treasury Secretary was publicly denying that he could.

These documents also reveal that Federal Reserve officials were incredulous and appalled that the Administration would make such statements because they ran a severe risk of panicking credit markets.

In 2001, I first introduced legislation to place an affirmative duty on the Treasury Department to provide first claim on any revenues for debt service. Ironically, the same Treasury Secretary who claimed he lacked legal authority opposed this bill that explicitly gave him that legal authority.

In response to his untruthful claim that it wasn't possible, we amended my bill in 2013 simply to allow the Treasury Secretary to borrow above the debt limit to guarantee that the debt would be paid in full and on time without having to prioritize. It passed the House in 2013, and again last year.

Opponents argued that this put creditors, like China, ahead of paying troops in the field. Actually, most of our debt is owed to Americans, and without our credit we can't pay our troops or anybody else. By protecting our credit first, we actually support and maintain our ability to pay for all of our other obligations.

Now, the President said this was tantamount to a family saying it would make its house payment, but not its car payment. Both are bad, but let us continue this analogy. If the family is living on its credit cards, as we are as a Nation, it had better make the minimum payments on its credit card first or it won't be able to pay the rest of its bills. And when that family has to increase its credit limit because it is spending above its means, it had better have a serious conversation about what is driving that debt and what to do about it.

Principled disputes over how the debt limit is addressed are going to happen from time to time. And just a few years ago, then-Senator Barack Obama vigorously opposed an increase in the debt limit sought by the Bush Administration. When these controversies erupt, as they inevitably do in a free society, it is imperative that credit markets are supremely confident that their loans to the United States are secure.

Thank you.

[The prepared statement of Representative McClintock can be found on page 57 of the appendix.]

Chairman DUFFY. Thank you, Congressman McClintock.

I would just note that votes have been called. There are 9 minutes on the clock. If this was in December, I would go to you, Mr. Pocan. But we have all realized that the new Speaker is calling votes after 15 minutes.

So with that, if you two don't mind coming back after votes, the subcommittee will stand in recess and will reconvene after this series of votes.

[recess]

Chairman DUFFY. The subcommittee will reconvene.

Just to be clear, without objection, the witnesses' written statements will be made a part of the record. And once the witnesses of the first panel have finished presenting their testimony, the chairman and the ranking member will each have 5 minutes to ask questions.

So with that, we will now go to the gentleman from the great State of Wisconsin, Mr. Pocan, for 5 minutes.

STATEMENT OF THE HONORABLE MARK POCAN, A REPRESENTATIVE IN CONGRESS FROM THE STATE OF WISCONSIN

Mr. POCAN. Great. Thank you very much, Mr. Chairman, Ranking Member Green, and members of the subcommittee.

Mr. Chairman, I just want to start out by saying that I think we can find bipartisan consensus on what you said at the beginning, that Wisconsin is the greatest State. So I just want to put that out there as a—

Chairman DUFFY. Hopefully, that is not where it ends.

Mr. POCAN. Yes. Just official suck-up to start.

Let me start with just a couple of things I want to put on your radar as we talk about this issue, and then let me address specifically the debt ceiling and the other issues that you are going to be talking about today.

I think it is important that we should note the Federal deficit has declined under President Obama by two-thirds since he came into office, and that is extremely significant and part of what we are looking at. In fact, this year the CBO has predicted the Federal deficit will increase very slightly after 6 consecutive years of decline, and that is due to our actions, what we did in December with the omnibus bill.

Not only did we provide some marginal sequester relief, but we had loads of retroactive tax cuts. And of course, none of those tax cuts were paid for; I think the last estimate I saw was they will cost about $680 billion over the next 10 years. And as of October last year, as a percentage of the economy, the deficit is now down to 2½ percent, which is below the average of the past half-century, and it is down about 9.8 percent since the President took office.

I just put those out there because I think they are significant as we talk about the subjects that we are talking about.

The second thing I just wanted to put out there for us to consider is the Simpson-Bowles Act that was out there, the proposal about how to try to provide relief—I know that I wasn't around; this is only my second term. But previously, when they were trying to find a grand bargain here in Congress and that couldn't happen, the Budget Control Act was put in place.

And if you look at what was in the Simpson-Bowles Act that people have referred to often, we have already enacted 70 percent of the non-defense discretionary cuts that were proposed by that Act. And according to the Center for a Responsible Budget, we have already cut 30 percent more discretionary spending than was proposed to be done by 2020 by Simpson-Bowles. All of those are programs that are important in our districts.

And yet, at the same time, we have enacted less than one-third of the proposed revenue changes that were also proposed by that. I just put that out there because as someone who has been a small-business owner for, this year it will be now 29 years, I look at that. A balance sheet is what we take in and what we put out. And I think that is significant because I don't think a lot of people realize what we have done on the taking out, but not necessarily the putting back in side of things.

Specifically to the debt ceiling, when I talk to people in my part of Wisconsin, I think it is no different than yours, Mr. Chairman, when I try to explain what the debt ceiling is about; it is essentially we have made a home mortgage, we have committed to that payment, and when we lift the debt ceiling, it is really whether or not we are going to put that in the mail.

And I think if you look at it as that, where the responsibility really is is up front where we decide whether or not we are going to make that decision, to make that spending, which is that home mortgage, rather than trying to deal with a debt limit when we often are putting ourselves in a pretty bad place.

As a small-business owner, I know what happens. Last time when we shut the government down, I did happen to be around for that. I saw what happened across the country when we lost billions of dollars out of the economy, when it affected small businesses and the decision-making they are going to make. It had a really negative effect.

And we have to be very careful when we put that out there as a tool, because I think all too often it has very negative ramifications. Our entire economy can be really rattled if we don't do the right thing. Millions of Americans could face delays in Social Security checks, veterans benefits, and other critical services. And it does put our country, I think, largely at risk.

In the minute remaining, let me just touch briefly on the debt prioritization that I think has been part of the conversation that you are having.

In many ways, I feel that the average person out there would look at this as somewhat of a ridiculous conversation, different than how we talk about things maybe in the Beltway. We need to pay our bills on time, period, and they expect that out of us. And the problem is that we haven't been doing that part of our jobs very well, so then this becomes a proposal that we need to look at.

Fitch's ratings agency has already indicated that delaying payments on other obligations while honoring interest and principal payments would trigger a credit rating review and possibly a credit rating downgrade. So by doing something like this, we actually risk not only the credit of the country, but also there are many people who are worthwhile people who would get payments, veterans, students, the elderly, and others, whom I think come into play.

I have 6 seconds left, so I will yield back at this point, but I will be glad to take any questions, Mr. Chairman.

[The prepared statement of Representative Pocan can be found on page 66 of the appendix.]

Chairman DUFFY. Thank you, Congressman Pocan.

The Chair now recognizes himself for 5 minutes for questions.

I would just note that, giving my friend from Wisconsin a little bit of pushback, we have increased our debt by $8 trillion. And we pay $255 billion a year just to service that debt. And I know that you look for a lot of revenue to spend in a lot of different programs. That is a lot of money that could go to building roads and bridges and helping poor people, that you are actually spending on servicing the debt. So I think this is a real problem that has really negative consequences for our constituents.

I would just also note that when we have looked at the Treasury's internal and secretive analysis, they were looking at prioritizing principal, interest, Social Security, and veterans benefits, so those folks would have been taken care of first.

But to you, Mr. McClintock. You have been working on this bill and have been a champion of it for a very long time. Are you surprised by the pushback that you are getting from the Administration and even from some folks across the aisle and then come to learn that they were doing exactly what you were talking about? Mr.

McCLINTOCK. Nothing surprises me about the mendacity of this Administration anymore. So I can't say I was shocked, just shocked that there was a dissembling going on.

But I will say this: Nobody advocates the Federal Government not paying any of its bills. That is not at issue here. Very bad things would happen if we were unable to pay any of those bills. That is not the issue here. It is not a question of taking out a mortgage and then not paying it, not putting the mortgage check in the mail, as my friend suggests.

Here is the point. If you are paying your home mortgage with your credit card, and that is essentially what this country is doing at the moment, you darn well better be sure that you pay the credit card first, the minimum payment, or your credit gets cut off and you can't pay your home mortgage or your car payment or the grocery bill, for that matter. That is what is at stake here.

And when credit markets begin to wonder if there is going to be a stalemate in Washington, the risk for making loans to the Federal Government goes up, the interest rates go up. And your point is spot on, our interest costs are already eating us alive, $255 billion this year just to rent the money we have already spent. We throw billion-dollar figures around here all the time without any reference point in the real world.

Every billion dollars is about $8 from an average family's taxes, which means that if you are an average family paying average taxes, about $2,000 of which you sent to the IRS this year did nothing more than rent the money we have already spent. That has to be brought under control.

But the first thing we have to do is be sure that our interest rates don't start to spiral because there is a perceived risk that the loans made to this government are not absolutely secure and sound.

Chairman DUFFY. And I would just note that the $255 billion on the $19 trillion is at historic low interest rates. Without even borrowing any more money, it is going to go up just with the increase in rates that are on our horizon. So I think it is important that we note that.

I can't imagine in a family, as you just mentioned, Mr. McClintock, a mom and dad and a couple of kids having some tension about whether or not they can balance their budget. And if dad says, "Let us not balance ever," and then mom says, "Listen, we have to be fiscally responsible," it is going to create tension between the two of them. And if the two of them actually agree that they are never going to pay it, but give it to the kids, I am sure the kids are going to get a little upset at that, too, and go, hey, it is going to create a dialogue. And I think that is what has happened here.

But the point really is, and per your legislation and what we found out within Treasury was, we are going to pay the principal and the interest. We want to make sure American sovereign debt is never in jeopardy. But there is going to be a larger conversation about how we spend.

And maybe to you, Mr. Pocan. I know that when the vote came up on Mr. McClintock's bill—I think my stats are right—almost every Democrat voted against it. And I hear your concern, I think you stated it well. But now knowing that Treasury was actually doing the very thing that Mr. McClintock was talking about, but saying something else publicly, I don't know if those who voted against it feel a little bit misrepresented by the Administration? And maybe if you were in line with the President and his view on Mr. McClintock's bill, maybe it would have been one of those bipartisan votes with 435 Members saying "aye" to Mr. McClintock's proposal.

Mr. POCAN. Yes, if I can, I think what I would offer is that I think the public looks at it differently. There is a reason why there is a 15 percent approval rating on Congress and they prefer traffic jams and zombies and head lice to us, right? They expect us to do our jobs. And we haven't done our jobs doing the process the way we are supposed to.

Now, I am looking forward to this new day we are going to have in Congress. I know we are having a more thorough, regular-order process. But if we don't do our basic jobs in getting a budget done, we can't come to the Band-Aid solutions, which is what we are doing here, and that is what this proposal unfortunately is.

So I think it comes down to the core of what we are supposed to do and what the public expects of us. And when we don't do our jobs, then we need to expect the public to prefer the things they prefer over us.

I guess that is my response, that we should really be dealing with what we need to deal with first and foremost, and these things are either side attractions or Band-Aids.

Chairman DUFFY. Thank you. My time has expired.

I now recognize the gentleman from Texas, Mr. Green, the ranking member of the subcommittee, for 5 minutes.

Mr. GREEN. Thank you very much, Mr. Chairman.

Of course, I thank my colleagues for being with us today. And I am grateful that you have given considerable thought to these questions.

I will have an opening statement that I will deliver at a later time, but I do think it important to note that I don't think you will find a Member of Congress who won't agree that we should pay our debts. I don't think you will find a Member of Congress who would say we should shut down the government.

However, I do know that there are Members of Congress who contend that you can make partial payments, and by making a partial payment you somehow cause everything to go on and you don't have a disruption in domestic markets and international markets.

The witnesses who will be testifying after my colleagues will indicate some of the concerns that they have with reference to disruptions of markets in the event we make a partial payment of our debts, partial payment meaning just decide to pay the principal and interest, take care of the Treasuries, make sure the bonds are paid, and overlook things like Medicaid, Medicare, and Social Security. There is at least one witness who thinks that we should overlook Social Security, just pay the interest on the debt.

So with that as the circumstance, Mr. Pocan, would you advocate in any way making a partial payment, meaning pay some parts of the debt, but not paying all of the debts?

Mr. POCAN. I think that is what is really at the point that we are having a debate about, whether or not, if we did our jobs right in the first place, we don't have to have this ancillary conversation later. And that is exactly, I think, what we are doing.

When I went through just my experience in that October when we were shut down for 17 days, people were very upset that we weren't doing our jobs. And it seemed like, I think there were 22 demands that came during the 17 days. I remember one morning watching Darrell Issa on TV addressing a demand, and they said, oh, no, your demands have changed already, now it is a different demand. And we tried to keep up with the demands that were made.

The bottom line is we just have to pay all of our bills. As you said, that is what the public expects of us, that is what we all want and need to do. But we have to be responsible and get that done.

And if we don't get it done and we get to the point that we sometimes use the debt ceiling as an excuse, even though we have already made the expenditures, we have already done that and we can't use the other to not drop that envelope in the mail after we have already signed up for the mortgage. So it is incumbent on us to get that done.

Mr. GREEN. I think it is also important that we give some definition to the term, "raise the debt ceiling." Because I think there is a nebulous notion in the minds of the public as to what this actually means.

It really means to pay the bills you have already incurred, that you have agreed to pay. Pay the bills that are owed and properly due as opposed to some notion that we are now trying to extend credit beyond some unreasonable amount. We are talking about money owed to people, in many cases doctors who will help us with Medicare and Medicaid, or money owed to businesses, but we are talking about paying what is owed.

That is what raising the debt ceiling means, that we are simply going to pay the debt that we already owe, in fact that Congress has agreed to pay. Is this a fair statement, Mr. Pocan?

Mr. POCAN. No, absolutely. That is the part that—maybe it is because I am still new around here and I go back to Wisconsin a lot, but that is what I hear from people when I talk to them. I try to bring Washington to them. I figure that is my job. And when you try to explain something like this, around here we have all sorts of things that just aren't "real people-speak." We have inside-the-Beltway conversations and this is one that is a classic.

If you agree to a home mortgage, you have to pay it; you can't decide not to because of something like we do with the debt ceiling. So that whole debate that we have is often to real people a very ridiculous debate that we wouldn't pay that; you have already authorized the expenditure. And then to have to have a Band-Aid solution because we didn't do our jobs to begin with is exactly what we are talking about.

Mr. GREEN. And if you have third parties that we owe money to and they are, let us call them a part of the international community, and they see us bickering about paying debts that are already owed, does that have an adverse impact on them, do you think?

Mr. POCAN. Yes, and it is not just us. It is the financial agencies that said that if we did that it would affect our credit rating, which would affect just about everything. I think it would have ripple effects throughout the economy, to businesses, to how we borrow, to everything else. So it does have real ramifications.

And while sometimes I think that some enjoy the dance, the fight that we have around here, real people back in Wisconsin whom I talk to don't.

Mr. GREEN. I thank you very much. And I will yield back. My time is up.

Chairman DUFFY. The gentleman yields back.

That concludes the opening statements and the questions for our first panel. I want to thank Congressman McClintock and Congressman Pocan for their testimony and insight today. And I would just note the witnesses are now excused.

We will now call our second panel as we make a transition here.

I want to welcome our second panel. Thank you for being here. What we are going to do is the Chair and the ranking member will make opening statements. We will then introduce and recognize each of you for your opening statements, and then we will go to questions.

So with that, the Chair now recognizes himself for 5 minutes for an opening statement.

Today's hearing is about unsustainable Federal spending and the credibility and trustworthiness of the Obama Administration on issues surrounding the debt limit. The United States is $19 trillion in debt and growing at a rate of over $3 billion a day.

The Federal Government spends $255 billion a year—$255 billion a year—just to service the interest on our debt. Spending at this rate is unsustainable and is the reason why so many of my colleagues and I actually ran for Congress. We cannot continue to tax and spend and borrow on the backs of our next generation.

The statutory debt limit established by Congress is a critical tool to keep our national debt in check and to protect taxpayers from runaway borrowing. In 2011, Congress challenged President Obama to address our Nation's debt by linking spending cuts to his request for a debt limit increase.

As Americans and people all over the world watched this political fight play out, whether it was on the nightly news or on other networks, in 2011, 2013, and 2015, Administration officials repeatedly told the public that chaos would cripple the global economy if the debt limit wasn't raised and that legislative proposals to reduce the impact of hitting the debt limit, such as prioritizing payments on the debt, should not be taken seriously.

We heard from officials, like Treasury Secretary Lew, former Deputy Secretary Neal Wolin, and former Assistant Secretary of Legislative Affairs Alastair Fitzpayne, that it would be "unworkable" for Congress to require the Treasury Department to prioritize principal and interest payments on the debt, and that the Administration had never made a decision to prioritize debt payments in the event the debt ceiling deal was not reached.

And as noted by the Financial Services Committee staff report, multiple Treasury officials, including Secretary Lew, have created the misleading impression that prioritizing principal and interest payments on the debt, such as which was suggested by key credit rating agencies, is not a serious option available to the Administration in the event the debt ceiling was not raised.

However, as revealed in the committee staff report, internal records of the New York Fed show that the Administration has been preparing debt ceiling contingency plans and running so-called tabletop exercises since at least 2011 that take into account various payment prioritization scenarios, including the prioritization of Social Security, veterans benefits, and principal and interest payments over other government obligations.

Moreover, these internal records reveal that the Administration in fact was planning to prioritize payments on the debt during the debt limit negotiations of 2013 in the event the debt ceiling was not raised.

Rather than being forthright with the American people and assuring the financial markets and the holders of U.S. Treasury notes that the U.S. Treasury notes would not be defaulted on and the United States would not default on its sovereign debt, the Obama Administration chose instead to mislead the public for the purpose of pressuring Congress to acquiesce to the Administration's no-negotiation position on the debt ceiling. Basically, they were playing politics.

The American people deserve and demand much better. Our Nation's creditworthiness should not be hindered by the Administration's lack of trustworthiness.

I look forward to discussing the committee's staff report today and exposing the truth behind the Administration's misleading claims concerning its debt ceiling contingency plans. And I also look forward to having a frank discussion about the ever-increasing debt that the Federal Government is accruing and putting on the backs of our children and our grandchildren. And I am also looking forward to the testimony and feedback from our panel.

With that, I conclude my remarks, and I recognize the gentleman from Texas, Mr. Green, the ranking member of the subcommittee, for 5 minutes.

Mr. GREEN. Thank you, Mr. Chairman.

I would like to thank these witnesses as well. And I would note that prioritizing debt, such as you pay P&I, principal and interest, is but another way to say "default." It really is.

It is a means by which we will honor obligations to some and default on obligations to others. And some of the witnesses on the Republican side have indicated that prioritizing and paying some debt is not preferable, that there are consequences.

And in fact, one witness—I have read all of the testimony, but one witness, and I am going to take a stab at your name, is it Ms. "de Rugy?"

Ms. DE RUGY. Yes.

Mr. GREEN. Okay. Ms. de Rugy—thank you—has indicated on page three of her testimony in the first full paragraph, to be sure, default should not be an option on the table. We will talk about that later. She also goes on to say that while Washington has difficult choices to make, defaulting on its debt obligations should not be part of the discussion about how to handle the debt limit or reduce long-term government spending.

So why are we talking about prioritizing debt? What is this leading up to? Well, I think a better name for this hearing today would be, "How to mislead voters away from legislation and toward confrontation." Because we are some 400-days-plus away from the debt ceiling, some 9,000-plus hours; there is plenty of time to deal with this debt ceiling without creating a crisis.

There is no pending crisis now, no impending crisis. And because there is no impending crisis, we have somehow concluded that we need to now strategize on how we can prioritize the debt such that we can later on create a crisis. This crisis that we are creating gets in the way of legislation.

The same witness, who is from George Mason University, has given the Majority an outline of what can be done to deal with the so-called debt ceiling and has indicated that there are several things that can be done and we should be pursuing the outline of what can be done. This is what some of your witnesses have indicated, that there are things that we can do to eliminate the possibility of having a debt ceiling that creates a confrontation.

So we should be engaged in legislation right now. We should be legislating Mr. McClintock's bill.

And finally this: The Majority has the control of both the House and the Senate. You indicated that if you could get control, you would do all of these things to deal with the debt ceiling, yet rather than deal with the legislative side of it, we are here today plotting a means by which we can have a partial default, and trying to convince the public that a partial default will in some way not be the equivalent of a default that would cause us to lose credit ratings, won't cause investors to conclude that Treasuries are not the best investment for them.

Just pay the principal and interest. And by the way, when you just pay the principal and interest, you will not be paying payments to small businesses and contractors and vendors, Medicare payments to doctors, Medicaid payments to doctors and health providers. We won't be paying for the school lunch programs. We won't be paying for the NIH grants that we have outstanding. We won't be paying the salaries and benefits to Federal employees. We won't be paying for tax refunds.

By making a partial payment, we then eliminate all of these other things that we are obligated to pay. So I don't think that this hearing is seriously about anything other than finding a clever way to default at some point in the future when the debt ceiling may become an issue because right now it has been suspended.

And I take the debt ceiling seriously. I take debt seriously. I think we ought to cut and I think we ought to increase revenue so as to avoid having to have a debt crisis that will be something that we can manage, but for some reason, today we are going to look the other way and misdirect.

I yield back.

Chairman DUFFY. The gentleman yields back.

We now welcome our second panel of witnesses. First, we go to Dr. Mitchell, a senior fellow at the Cato Institute who specializes in fiscal policy.

Next, Dr. "de Rugy"—do I have that right, or close enough?

Ms. DE RUGY. Yes, close enough.

Chairman DUFFY. Okay. There was much discussion on how we say your name, so if I am close, good. Dr. de Rugy is a senior research fellow at the Mercatus Center at George Mason University, and a nationally syndicated columnist.

Next, Ms. "Boccia"—is that right?

Ms. BOCCIA. It is "Boccia," but thank you.

Chairman DUFFY. Okay. Ms. Boccia is the deputy director of the Thomas A. Roe Institute for Economics and Policy Studies, and a Grover M. Hermann research fellow at the Heritage Foundation.

And finally, Dr. Stone is a chief economist at the Center on Budget and Policy Priorities, where he specializes in the economic analysis of budget and policy issues.

To all of you, welcome.

You see you have three lights at your desks: the green light means go; the yellow light means that you have one minute left; and the red light means your time is up. Your microphones are sensitive, so you have to make sure you have them on when you speak, as a reminder.

And so with that, Dr. Mitchell, you are recognized for 5 minutes for your opening statement.

STATEMENT OF DANIEL J. MITCHELL, SENIOR FELLOW, THE CATO INSTITUTE

Mr. MITCHELL. Thank you, Mr. Chairman, and members of the subcommittee. My name is Dan Mitchell, and I am a senior fellow at the Cato Institute. I appreciate the opportunity to summarize my testimony here.

Our Nation faces very serious, long-run fiscal challenges thanks to changing demographics and poorly designed entitlement programs. All of you know that from various reports from CBO, OMB, GAO, and private forecasters. I would say all these estimates that we get tend to focus on the red ink, which I think is useful information, but I also think it is incomplete because what we should be focusing on is the underlying burden of government spending. The red ink is the symptom, and excessive government spending is the underlying problem. And that spending, whether it is financed by taxes, borrowing, or printing money, is what entails to a diversion of resources from the productive sector of the economy.

It is also best to focus on government spending because projections of ever-larger levels of long-run debt are the result of ever-expanding amounts of Federal spending, not inadequate tax receipts.

If you look at the CBO numbers that just came out, it is very clear that tax revenues already are above their long-run average, and not only that, but they are going to continue to increase over time, not because of legislated tax increases, but simply because some parts of the Tax Code aren't indexed to inflation, and also even low levels of economic growth will result in what is called real bracket creep over time.

So when you are looking 1 decade, 2 decades, 3 decades down the road, Federal tax revenue will be growing as a share of the economy. The problem that we have with our long-run fiscal forecast is not on the revenue side of the equation. Revenues are growing, but the burden of government spending is growing even faster.

And as I mentioned before, it is largely because of entitlement programs combined with changing demographics. A reasonable-sized welfare state is possible when you have a traditional population pyramid. But because of aging population and falling birthrates, we are moving toward a population cylinder, and that is going to create very, very serious problems. Indeed, if you look at some of these forecasts, we are on a path to becoming a failed European-style welfare state.

As a matter of fact, if you look at some of the long-run numbers, not only from our own agencies, but if you look at what the International Monetary Fund is projecting, the Organization for Economic Cooperation and Development, the Bank for International Settlements, they all show numbers that are actually worse than what you see in terms of the long-run forecasts for France, Italy, Greece, and places like that.

Now, I actually think those estimates are a little bit too pessimistic because they are basically premised on the notion that we have this big, built-in increase in government spending and tax revenues are growing only very slowly as a share of the economy and they assume compounding levels of government debt.

We could actually solve that problem relatively simply by simply putting a cap on government spending. And so, even though these long-run forecasts show us with more long-run debt than France and Greece and Italy, I actually think our problem is much easier to solve because they are already at levels where the government is consuming more than half of the productive sector of the economy, and their tax burdens are at or above the revenue-maximizing level. That is a much, much harder problem to solve.

We do have this long-run problem, so the question is, however you measure it, how do we solve it? Should the debt limit be an action-forcing event for fiscal reform?

And my conclusion is yes, because it beats the alternative. And here is an example that I shared with the Senate Budget Committee a couple of years ago. Look at Greece today, a very deep recession, a completely miserable economic situation, incredibly high levels of unemployment, including 50 percent unemployment for young people. Why are they in this mess? Because they had a fiscal crisis.

Imagine, though, if 15 or 20 or 25 years ago Greece had something akin to the debt limit, some action-forcing event. And let us say that some lawmakers 15 or 20 or 25 years ago threw sand in the gears, caused shutdowns, caused debt limit fights, whatever you want to call it, but imagine if all that had forced Greece to engage in reform. It might have caused a little bit of discomfort then, but it would have saved the Greek people from the much, much deeper levels of misery that they are suffering now.

And I sort of view the whole debt limit fights or government shutdown fights, any of the fights that we are having now, sequester fights, they are basically an opportunity to save America from enduring that kind of suffering that the Greek people are dealing with. And so that is why a debt limit fight or some other fight would be necessary.

Now there are, of course, arguments against this approach. One of the arguments is, and we saw this with the July 2015 GAO report, that, oh, if you have these debt limit fights, what is going to happen? You are going to have higher levels of interest on the debt. Again, that is peanuts compared to the long-term suffering that might occur.

And the other argument is that you are going to have a default or you are not going to be able to pay interest on the debt.

I will close with simply the point that in 2017, the next time we have a debt limit, CBO projects that revenues will be more than $3.5 trillion and they project that interest on the debt will be $308 billion, more than 11 times as much revenue as would be needed. So prioritization, not desirable, but it would work.

Thank you.

[The prepared statement of Dr. Mitchell can be found on page 59 of the appendix.]

Chairman DUFFY. The gentleman yields back.

The Chair now recognizes Dr. de Rugy for 5 minutes.

STATEMENT OF VERONIQUE DE RUGY, SENIOR RESEARCH FELLOW, MERCATUS CENTER, GEORGE MASON UNIVERSITY

Ms. DE RUGY. Thank you, Mr. Chairman.

Chairman Duffy, Ranking Member Green, and members of the subcommittee, thank you for the opportunity to testify before you today. My name is Veronique de Rugy, and I am a senior research fellow at the Mercatus Center.

I would like to make three points today. First, since the debt limit showdown of 2011 and 2013, we have come a long way in understanding how the debt ceiling works and what are the options available for us the next time there is a crisis.

Second, we still need to recognize that these fights that we are having over the debt ceiling are actually just a symptom of a much more problematic problem, and that is government's overspending. It is because the government year after year spends more than it should, that it needs to constantly or regularly at least increase its borrowing authority.

This state of affairs is not sustainable. And we need to address the explosion of spending on the programs that are the drivers of our future debt.

Thankfully, we actually have a lot of policy solutions available, either institutional reform or entitlement reform, that have been proposed over the years. And we can implement them to actually create a check on government spending.

So, let me start. During the last debt ceiling debate in 2011, my colleague Jason Fechner and I wrote a paper that explained that when the government reaches the debt ceiling, and then Treasury can no longer issue Federal debt, it would still have ways to stave off a regrettable default, by which I mean not paying interest on the debt and the principal.

Using these techniques would give Congress time to reach an agreement about how to implement fundamental-type reform that would get us on a more sustainable fiscal path.

At the time, we explained that, for instance, Treasury had several financial management options to continue paying the government's obligation, including but not only prioritizing payments, liquidating some assets to pay government bills and using the Social Security Trust Fund to continue paying Social Security benefits.

At the time, we were told that these were not acceptable or possible options. This is why yesterday I was really glad to read this committee's report which actually shows that indeed Treasury has the ability to prioritize payment, including interest on the debt and principal and Social Security payments. And that even in 2013, the Federal Reserve of New York was actually running tabletop exercises to prepare for such contingencies.

Now, it is important to note that we were never advocating any particular measure. More importantly, we often lamented that this path had to be pursued because of the irresponsibility of government. However, we noted that it was much more reasonable than defaulting on our debt or raising the debt ceiling without making any fundamental changes to the state of our finances. That is what Presidents and Congresses have done for decades.

The debt ceiling was raised 20 times since 1993 and the result is a growing government and a Federal debt that has ballooned from less than $5 trillion to $19 trillion. And deficits are also going up according to the recent Congressional Budget Office report.

Over the coming decade, the size of the Federal deficit will double to reach a gap of almost 5 percent of GDP. CBO predicts that deficits will total $9.4 trillion over 10 years. That is up from $1.5 trillion since its August report. And according to Treasury, unfunded liabilities average $75.5 trillion.

As Will Rogers once said, "If you find yourself in a hole, stop digging." The government, too, needs to stop digging. That is true now, but it also is going to be important the next time you have a debate about raising the debt ceiling.

Real institutional reform as opposed to one-time cuts would change the trajectory of fiscal policy and put the United States on a more sustainable path. I believe we should adopt a constitutional amendment to limit spending, but there are reforms that could be implemented immediately, such as ending the abuse of the emergency spending label, adopting a strict cut-as-you-go system, or creating a BRAC-like commission for discretionary spending.

Finally, Congress must have the courage to implement real entitlement reform to curtail spending on Medicare, Medicaid, the Affordable Care Act subsidy, and Social Security. Without reform today, vast tax increases will be needed to pay for unfunded promises made to a steadily growing cohort of seniors.

Fortunately, many workable solutions are available to lawmakers, including adding a system of personal savings accounts to Social Security, liberalizing medical savings accounts and making the latter permanent to reduce health care costs by increasing competition between providers and making consumers more responsive.

So thank you, and I am ready for your questions.

[The prepared statement of Dr. de Rugy can be found on page 51 of the appendix.]

Chairman DUFFY. Thank you.

The Chair now recognizes Ms. Boccia for 5 minutes.

STATEMENT OF ROMINA BOCCIA, DEPUTY DIRECTOR, THOMAS A. ROE INSTITUTE FOR ECONOMIC POLICY STUDIES, AND GROVER M. HERMANN RESEARCH FELLOW, THE HERITAGE FOUNDATION

Ms. BOCCIA. Chairman Duffy, Ranking Member Green, and members of the Subcommittee on Oversight and Investigations, thank you for having me here to testify today.

My name is Romina Boccia, I am the Grover Hermann research fellow in Federal budgetary affairs, and deputy director at the Roe Institute in the Heritage Foundation. The views I express in this testimony are my own and should not be construed as representing any official position of the Heritage Foundation.

The Nation is on a fiscal collision course. Absent presidential and congressional leadership through the regular budget process, the debt limit is a key action-forcing tool that drives the attention towards our Nation's precarious fiscal state and enables lawmakers to leverage a potential crisis scenario for necessary and urgent policy reforms that might not otherwise come about.

Though the debt limit may be a blunt tool to motivate fiscal discipline, leveraging it to enact structural reforms that rein in growing spending and debt may very well prevent a much worse fiscal crisis. Contrast debt limit negotiations with an unexpected, sudden, and drastic fiscal crisis that would leave policymakers with few tools to respond in a predictable and gradual manner.

The latest fiscal and economic projections by the Congressional Budget Office paint a very clear picture. Spending and debt are growing at an unsustainable pace, greatly increasing the risks of a sudden fiscal crisis during which investors would demand much higher interest rates to continue lending to the U.S. Government. Congress should prevent such a scenario by reforming those programs that drive the growth in spending and the debt before increasing the debt limit.

Moreover, growing spending is driving debt to increasingly economically harmful levels. Projected deficits would push debt held by the public to 86 percent of GDP by the end of the decade, or about twice the historical average level. Several analysts and pundits argue that the debt limit is an archaic construct which serves no useful purpose. They argue that because Congress authorizes all spending, it does not make sense to have a separate limit on borrowing.

I disagree. Ideally, congressional decisions to spend and borrow would be aligned. However, there are at least three reasons why the debt limit serves a useful purpose. First, the programs driving the majority of the growth in Federal spending were authorized many decades ago and they are now allowed to grow on autopilot with few congressional action-forcing deadlines to change those programs' trajectories.

Second, the public, as we know from polling, does not recognize that it is their most cherished entitlement programs that are driving the growth in spending and the debt and the debt limit can help elevate public understanding while at the same time providing important political cover for lawmakers who seek to reduce spending on those entitlements.

Third, lawmakers only control some of the factors that drive the growth in the debt. And economic downturns or unanticipated increases in interest costs may mean that previously authorized spending should be reconsidered in light of factors outside of Congress' control. The government should pay its bills, but it should also adjust commitments going forward.

As the Federal Government approaches the debt limit, and absent congressional action to increase the limit, Treasury does not necessarily default on debt obligations. Treasury can reasonably be expected to prioritize principal and interest payments on the national debt, protecting the full faith and credit of the United States of America above all other spending.

Sovereign debt default should never be a primary concern during a temporary debt limit impasse. Congress has voted in support of several bills that would allow Treasury to continue borrowing at the debt limit to meet debt service needs.

In the event that insufficient cash levels became a concern to meet Federal debt obligations, Congress and the Administration could immediately act to remove at least this critical risk. Moreover, each year congressional budget committees and the Executive Branch should prepare a prioritized annual cash budget. This would be a prudent exercise to reveal to the public what Congress and the Executive Branch consider to be the most important national programs.

It would also confront lawmakers and the public more directly with the important questions of whether the things the Federal Government is currently borrowing for are truly necessary. In the event of a debt limit impasse, this cash budget could serve as guidance for prioritization of payments at the debt limit.

The debt limit provides an important action-forcing deadline to pursue the legislative steps necessary to rein in out-of-control entitlement spending. The debt limit also provides political leverage to pursue those reforms necessary to change the debt trajectory and restore economic growth to its full potential.

Thank you.

[The prepared statement of Ms. Boccia can be found on page 40 of the appendix.]

Chairman DUFFY. Thank you.

And the Chair now recognizes Dr. Stone for 5 minutes.

STATEMENT OF CHAD STONE, CHIEF ECONOMIST, CENTER ON BUDGET AND POLICY PRIORITIES

Mr. STONE. Thank you.

Chairman Duffy, Ranking Member Green, and members of the subcommittee, thank you for the opportunity to testify at today's hearing.

In my written testimony, I make two broad points. The first is the need to focus not just on spending, but also on revenues in addressing our long-term budget challenges.

The second is to caution strongly against thinking that the statutory limit on Federal debt has a constructive role to play in addressing those challenges.

Budget deficits result from an imbalance between spending and revenue, rising debt relative to the size of the economy results from persistent large deficits, not from too much spending, per se. Any plausible amount of spending to meet society's needs is sustainable if there are sufficient revenues to avoid large deficits.

CBO projects that under current tax and spending policies, rising debt will ultimately prove unsustainable. This poses a serious challenge to policymakers. At the same time, as I discuss in the first part of my testimony, there is not an immediate crisis. Policymakers, however, will have to make hard choices in setting a future course that is both fiscally responsible and realistic about the levels of spending and taxes appropriate to the country's needs. These decisions need to be kept separate from the debt limit.

As I discussed in the second part of my testimony, the debt limit encourages reckless brinkmanship that makes it harder to work out the compromises necessary to achieve a sustainable deficit reduction agreement. As former Federal Reserve Chairman Ben Bernanke says in his recent book, refusing to raise the debt limit takes the economic well-being of the country hostage. That ought to be unacceptable, no matter what underlying issue is being contested.

Here are some key points from my written testimony, that I will be happy to elaborate on later. On trends in government spending and debt, which I will always speak of relative to the size of the economy, i.e., as a share of GDP rather than in dollar terms, I have four charts in my testimony that help illustrate the following points.

First, the financial crisis and the Great Recession were a major shock to the economy and the budget. But factors causing a surge in deficits and debt after 2008 were temporary revenue losses and spending increases due to the economic weakness and temporary tax cuts and spending increases to combat that weakness.

Those policies have largely abated as the economy has been recovering. Stimulus programs have phased down and policymakers have enacted new deficit-reduction policies.

Second, budget analysts have known for a long time that the aging of the population and rising health care costs are the drivers of long-term spending projections, not a problem of spending growing faster than the economy throughout the government.

The Center on Budget and Policy Priorities finds, for example, that program, that is non-interest, spending outside of Social Security and Medicare, is running below its historical average as a percent of GDP and is projected to fall further in the future.

Increasing generosity of benefits is not what is driving the increase in Social Security and Medicare spending. Rather, it is the rising share of the population eligible for benefits, and in Medicare rising health care costs, which affect public and private health care spending alike.

Historical levels of spending and revenues are a poor guide to what is required to meet 21st Century national needs and be fiscally responsible.

Third, and this is important, low-income programs are not a driver of long-term deficit projections. Specifically, outside of health care, Federal spending for low-income programs, including refundable tax credits, such as the earned income tax credit, are on track to fall below their 4-decade average of 2.1 percent of GDP in coming years—fall below.

Fourth, long-run fiscal sustainability does not require balanced budgets. For example, even though there were deficits in almost every year between World War II and the early 1970s, debt grew much more slowly than the economy, so the debt-to-GDP ratio fell dramatically.

Let me be brief about the debt limit. Setting a limit on debt is an ineffective means of controlling deficits. That is a direct quote from a 2010 CBO report. Debt subject to a statutory limit is a measure that has no economic or financial significance. CBO instead features debt held by the public, basically the sum of all past deficits minus surpluses, in its presentations because that public borrowing is what affects national saving and credit markets.

The debt limit is not innocuous if it is used politically and raises concerns that the United States might actually do the unthinkable and default on its financial obligations. It is not innocuous. Debt prioritization measures, like the ones we are talking about, do not mitigate that problem, even if it proves feasible to pull out and pay interest and Social Security obligations.

By appearing to make a default legitimate and manageable, it would heighten the risk that one would actually occur. Failing to pay other obligations in a protracted showdown would be like sequestration on steroids and would be damaging to the United States credit rating.

Thank you.

[The prepared statement of Dr. Stone can be found on page 68 of the appendix.]

Chairman DUFFY. Thank you.

The Chair now recognizes himself for 5 minutes.

This is really a hearing about Treasury and Treasury's, I would argue, dishonesty with this committee, this Congress, and with the American people.

We had been talking about their need to prioritize debt payments or U.S. obligations. And they basically told the American people and us that this was unworkable when in fact they had a program in place to do just what we were talking about. And I would argue they were doing that for political reasons, to try to put the financial markets in turmoil over this spending fight that we are having.

They have an obligation to be honest with this committee. And even now, the records that we have have come from the New York Fed. The Treasury has been less than compliant with this committee about their internal deliberations. And even when they send us documents, they try to thwart us by sending it in a format that we cannot print and we cannot search. This is not open and this is not transparent.

I look to the ranking member. I would be delighted if we did not have to have any debates about spending because we had Barack Obama and my friends across the aisle who got it and said we have too much money going in current obligations and future obligations, we have to reform our budgets and our spending so there is no need to even talk about the debt limit. That would be beautiful, but that is not what is happening.

We don't get to buy-in. And the bottom line is, to get a bill done you need the House, the Senate, and the President. So we need these tools to actually reform the way that we spend to save us, Dr. Mitchell, from a Greece-like scenario right here in America.

When financial crises happen, and maybe, Dr. Mitchell, to you, to Greece, were the millionaires in Greece the worst-hurt from their crisis, or was it the poorest among the Greece population who were hurt from their financial crisis?

Mr. MITCHELL. If you look at the data in Greece, the unemployment rate, the actual, genuine spending cuts, not just spending cuts off a baseline, but the actual spending cuts that Greece has been forced to make, that was the thrust of my presentation. If you wait too long, if you keep kicking the can down the road, when the crisis eventually does occur it is much, much more serious.

So that is why I think whatever short-term hiccup we have because we are fighting over a debt limit or something like that is a much easier and lower price to pay than the kinds of very negative consequences that the Greek people, especially low-income Greek people, have suffered as a result of the crisis.

Chairman DUFFY. I would agree. The poorest community in a society, who rely on their government for help, are the ones who will be hurt the worst if a crisis comes. So to tell those in need of government help, don't worry, we are going to give you all that you want and even more than you want for 5, 10, 20 years, but then have a debt crisis and not be able to help them out, I think is disingenuous and dishonest.

And frankly, talking about how this institution works, it is concerning for us that the other side doesn't talk about restraining spending, they just talk about more programs, more offerings, and more spending as opposed to spending restraint.

Chairman DUFFY. Dr. Stone, did you say that this debt limit situation and negotiation in the House was reckless? Was that your testimony?

Mr. STONE. Risking default is reckless, yes.

Chairman DUFFY. So is it fair to say that you are calling Barack Obama reckless in 2006 when he said, "The fact that we are here today to debate America's debt limit is a sign of leadership failure; it is a sign that the U.S. Government can't pay its own bills." He was in favor of using the debt limit to adjust how America spends.

Are you saying that Barack Obama is reckless?

Mr. STONE. I am saying that over history the existence of the debt limit has caused politicians to make, in voting on it on both sides, to make statements like that, but we reached a new level when we were using it to threaten shutting down the government as opposed to—

Chairman DUFFY. So you would agree with me that your statement is calling Barack Obama reckless when he was advocating for the same policies that we have advocated for in spending restraint, using the power of the purse of this institution? Yes?

Mr. STONE. Demanding that the debt limit be raised as—look—

Chairman DUFFY. Yes?

Mr. STONE. Yes, for all politicians who have used the debt limit, but it is a careless statement. But in circumstances where it is not meant to lead to a shutdown of the government, it is less reckless.

Chairman DUFFY. Ms. Boccia, and I only have a few seconds left, do you think it is appropriate that the Congress try to restrain spending by using all tools possible to get a consensus about getting us on a trajectory that is sustainable in regard to our spending and our debt?

Ms. BOCCIA. I think it is very much appropriate. I think Congress must use all the tools in its arsenal to rein in growing spending and debt. And to those who say it is okay, we will just raise taxes, the problem we have is that spending is growing much faster than the economy. And in the long run, you cannot raise taxes faster than the economy is growing. It is going to be impossible, which is why the CBO says this scenario is unsustainable.

And the debt limit, I think, is a critical tool to bring about reforms before a sudden fiscal crisis ties Congress' hands.

Chairman DUFFY. Thank you.

My time has expired.

The Chair now recognizes the gentlelady from Ohio, Mrs. Beatty, for 5 minutes.

Mrs. BEATTY. Thank you, Mr. Chairman, and Ranking Member Green.

I am going to be very brief and just make a statement I would like to be entered into the record, and a question. And if appropriate, I would like to yield the balance of my time to the ranking member.

My statement for the record is that in that this is a formal hearing, I would appreciate, as we say "chairman" and "Dr." and "Mr." that we make reference to the President of these United States as President Barack Obama in this hearing. That is just my personal statement.

Secondly, my question is yesterday, the Majority released a press release in which I believe the chairman of this subcommittee was quoted as saying that President Barack Obama manufactured a crisis when talking about the consequences of raising the debt limit in 2011.

Dr. Stone, do you believe that the President manufactured a crisis?

Mr. STONE. I don't.

Mrs. BEATTY. Do you believe that failure to raise the debt limit is an actual crisis?

Mr. STONE. Failing to raise the debt limit when it comes due, and when there are obligation to be paid, can create a crisis, yes.

Mrs. BEATTY. Thank you.

Mr. Chairman, I would like to yield the balance of my time to Ranking Member Green.

Mr. GREEN. I thank the gentlelady.

And let us start with this notion that you have to have the House and the Senate and the President to legislate. That didn't stop us from voting more than 50 times to repeal the Affordable Care Act without the House and the Senate and the President. Legislate, you are in the Majority now. Do what the Majority should do and has a responsibility to do. Legislate!

Pass Mr. McClintock's bill. I know what it does. But then you will have legitimized that process.

What you want to do is have the Administration legitimize a process that has severe consequences so that you can continue to blame Barack Obama.

And I yield to myself the notion that I should say, "President Barack Obama." And I am going to do that, but I had to do that for emphasis.

This is what it is all about. You have witnesses on your side who have indicated that we should not default. Let us test this. If you think we should default on the debt, raise your hand. Let the record reflect that no one has raised a hand. They don't think we should default.

Now, Mr. Stone, prioritizing and paying P&I only, is that a form of default?

Mr. STONE. We are not meeting all of our obligations. Under the Constitution, we have a debt limit and we have the requirement to meet all of our financial obligations. They are in conflict.

Mr. GREEN. So that is a form of default, all right.

Let me ask my other friends on the panel. What do you call paying P&I only, not taking care of Social Security, not taking care of military obligations, not taking care of Medicaid and Medicare? What do you call the failure to take care of those things?

And I will start with the lady that I called on earlier, Ms. de Rugy.

Ms. DE RUGY. I call that scare tactics.

Mr. GREEN. Let me ask you this—

Ms. DE RUGY. In 2013 and 2011—

Mr. GREEN. —if I may intercede, please, since I have the time. You call it scare tactics. Let me ask you this. You call default only if you don't pay P&I. That is your definition of default, I see, because if you thought that failure to pay P&I is default, then you would have to conclude that you are defaulting on those obligations as well. You can't conclude that only principal and interest is a part of our obligations. All of these other things are obligations, too.

If you think that we only have an obligation to pay P&I, raise your hand. Nobody thinks that we only have an obligation to pay P&I. Let the record reflect that no one raised a hand.

So this is really about trying to find a clever way to avoid making payments, have the Administration do it, not pass legislation to get it done. You have the Majority. Pass the legislation. Pass Mr. McClintock's bill. Pass other legislation.

You have been given five things that you can do short of creating a debt crisis, short of defaulting. Five things that Ms. de Rugy has indicated we can do, five, and they don't require a default. Is that a correct statement, Ms. de Rugy?

Ms. DE RUGY. I don't—

Mr. GREEN. Do any of these require default, the five things that you have given us?

Ms. DE RUGY. These are like suggested fundamental reforms—

Mr. GREEN. I understand. But do any of your suggestions require default?

Ms. DE RUGY. —that Congress should agree on some of them.

Mr. GREEN. So you are saying your suggestions will require default?

Ms. DE RUGY. Default defined as paying interest on the debt?

Mr. GREEN. Default defined as not paying obligations.

Ms. DE RUGY. Absolutely not.

Mr. GREEN. Okay. So you have these five things that your witness has said you can do. You can do these things. You are in the Majority. Behave like you are in the Majority, legislate, don't try to create some sort of false, phony charade indicating that you are trying to prevent a debt ceiling crisis when in fact that is what you are going to do by prioritizing.

Chairman DUFFY. The gentleman yields back.

The Chair now recognizes the gentleman from Illinois, Mr. Hultgren, for 5 minutes.

Mr. HULTGREN. Thank you, Mr. Chairman.

Thank you all for being here. This is a very important subject, as we see ticking behind your heads and on the sides here. This is a huge challenge that we need to address, and we need to face. And I really do want to thank the witnesses for appearing here today.

I especially wanted to thank our previous panel. Congressman McClintock has shown incredible leadership on this issue. I am proud to be a cosponsor of the Default Prevention Act and was pleased to see it passed last October. I hope we can continue to push on that.

I have been more than frustrated with the Administration's apparent desire to increase our debt, and their disinterest in having serious conversations about reducing long-term spending, such as making reforms to our entitlement programs that we all know need to be discussed.

My first question I am going to address to Dr. Mitchell and maybe if somebody else wants to jump in as well.

But as we learned from the committee's report, the Administration is able to prioritize debt payments. In fact, they made plans to do so, but failed to share them with Congress and the American people.

Given the fact that Treasury is capable of prioritizing debt payments over other obligations, wouldn't it make sense for Congress to mandate that debt payments should be prioritized in the event the debt ceiling is reached, to ensure that America does not default on its sovereign debt?

Mr. MITCHELL. Two things, sir. Presumably, legislation wouldn't be needed because I am sure Treasury, if push came to shove, would prioritize because no Treasury Secretary would actually want to have default. And it is important to underscore that default, that paying P&I first doesn't mean that you are "defaulting" on other obligations. It simply means that they are being postponed.

Which brings up my second point. Plenty of State and local governments already do this. If States that are considered chronically mismanaged, like California, manage to prioritize at times when they run into their own fiscal challenges, I am sure that Treasury has all the expertise it would need to prioritize as well.

Mr. HULTGREN. Can I ask you a question on this just to clarify? Because I think so much of our economy is confidence-driven. It is consumer confidence. And so it really goes back to, by doing something like this this, it is sending a message out there that you don't have to worry, this is taken care of, we have the resources to pay for it.

So although you might be right in saying we can do this, I just think it sends that clear message that we will do this, that we are going to make sure that we are going to protect the American people, that our credit is important, that we are going to pay our bills. So I want to just—and maybe—

Mr. MITCHELL. I definitely think it would be good to pass the legislation, even though, in reality, I think Treasury would do the right thing anyhow.

Mr. HULTGREN. So we could do it. But by passing it, it just kind of makes that very clear. And I think it adds to that consumer confidence. And we have seen these threats, we have seen people abuse it, quite honestly on both sides, to push things through quickly without having the proper discussion or debate.

Dr. de Rugy, did you have any thoughts on that?

Ms. DE RUGY. No. I agree. But I also think a lot of the time it is like a false debate, because it is implied that all that the government can do or Treasury can do at a time of reaching the debt ceiling is pay P&I. And what we have seen time and again is actually there is enough revenue not only to pay P&I, but also to pay other obligations.

We have also seen, because it has been written up by GAO and it has been fact checked many times during the 2011 debate, that actually they could pay Social Security. And this is what I meant by scare tactics.

So the idea that all we could do is P&I is usually, actually, a false debate. Of course, if we reached a point where P&I is so big because we have let the government grow so far, then we have bigger problems.

Mr. HULTGREN. Let me flip it around really quick. There is, I guess, agreement that there is flexibility already there. There is ability and some misinformation, I think, of what the Treasury can do and can't do.

I guess to flip the question around, is there any valid reason for not supporting legislation instructing the Administration to prioritize payments to avoid defaulting on the Nation's sovereign debt? Wouldn't it be irresponsible not to do this in the event that the debt ceiling were reached?

Ms. DE RUGY. I guess no, it would actually end the debate.

Mr. HULTGREN. Yes?

Mr. STONE. I don't think you would end the debate. Yes, Treasury has the ability to manage various things for a short period of time once the limit is formally reached. And yes, you could meet some of the obligations by paying principal and interest, but in a protracted shutdown, in a protracted situation, you would be not meeting other obligations and that doesn't inspire confidence when the rest of the world and creditors see people not getting paid.

Mr. HULTGREN. My time has pretty much expired.

Did you have one last thing to say?

Ms. BOCCIA. I think it will be tremendously helpful to have congressional guidance to give investors confidence. I also would urge Congress to mandate that the Executive Branch put together a prioritized cash budget to show exactly how a prioritized budget would work in the event of a debt limit impasse.

Mr. HULTGREN. Yes, I think that is a good idea.

My time has expired. I yield back. Thanks, Mr. Chairman.

Chairman DUFFY. The gentleman yields back.

The Chair now recognizes the gentleman from Washington, Mr. Heck, for 5 minutes.

Mr. HECK. Thank you, Mr. Chairman.

I would like to begin my questions with a statement. I find all of this to be a bit surreal. And I will stipulate that is no doubt, in no small part, due to being raised in a household where mom and dad said, pay your bills.

I have to say that this whole idea of blowing through the debt ceiling and prioritizing or defaulting or however you want to characterize it absolutely reminds me of a couple getting in an argument about how high their credit card bill has become, and somebody says, well, this is easy, tear up the bill, as opposed to the credit card. And that is, in effect, what is being suggested here today by many people.

But not by everybody. In fact, I want to acknowledge that both Dr. de Rugy and Ms. Boccia had what I would characterize as the intellectual honesty to actually come out and say we need to cut Social Security in order to bring spending into line. And I think that is intellectually honest and I do commend you for it.

Dr. Mitchell, I heard you say that we needed to reduce spending, we needed to reduce entitlements. Are you ready to throw in with your colleagues that that includes Social Security and that the way to control spending going forward, it is your position, includes cutting Social Security benefits?

Mr. MITCHELL. If you look at the just-released CBO report, we could balance the budget by 2026 if we simply limit the growth of spending to 2.5 percent a year. The problem, of course, is on the baseline, spending is projected to grow more than 4 percent a year. So we are not talking about cutting necessarily, although there are plenty of programs and departments that should be cut, we are talking about limiting the aggregate growth of spending that is paid within that limit.

Mr. HECK. So it is pain-free?

Mr. MITCHELL. No, it is not pain-free at all. The interest groups would squeal if all of a sudden they were put on a diet, but that is exactly what things like a debt limit theoretically would do, force debate.

Mr. HECK. Reclaiming my time, Dr. de Rugy and Ms. Boccia, thank you for your intellectual honesty.

Dr. Stone, it seems to me that we are talking about this in kind of a hypothetical construct about what would happen, what could happen. And as it turns out, it seems to me this doesn't have to be a discussion about a hypothetical.

I am reminded of a government that is unable to pay its bills right now. It does in fact have enough money to pay the interest to its bondholders, but not enough to pay all of its obligations, and that is Puerto Rico.

I am trying to figure out what is the fundamental distinction between what is being proposed here, namely blowing through the debt limit and "prioritizing" and rendering ourselves Puerto Rico II. Is there any meaningful distinction between what they are having to go through? And does that make us seem as though we would be defaulting on our debt if we wanted to be like Puerto Rico?

Mr. STONE. Actually, there is a distinction. And in talking about Puerto Rico, and talking about Greece, that is not who we should be talking about when we are talking about the United States situation. We should be talking about Japan, which has a debt to GDP ratio of 200 percent and has no trouble borrowing.

The question is, how do financial markets react? Yes, down the road when U.S. debt to GDP is 400 percent, maybe we will have a financial crisis.

Mr. HECK. But my point, I think, Dr. Stone, is there isn't anybody who would look at Puerto Rico and say they are not on the verge of defaulting.

Mr. STONE. That is right.

Mr. HECK. And if we were to do what is proposed here today, we would be defaulting.

Mr. STONE. But we would be defaulting in the sense of not paying obligations because we were honoring a debt ceiling that we imposed on ourselves. That is why the family analogy doesn't make any sense.

Families can set a credit card limit, and if the kid gets sick and they need to spend more they can raise it. It is not the credit card company cutting off families.

Mr. HECK. Back to the credit card analogy, before my time expires, there has been a fairly cavalier use of the term "dishonesty" here today, which I want to take exception to, because I think it speaks to character. There can be issues of lack of consistency and the like.

But I guess it is in the eye of the beholder, because the truth of the matter is that this institution is governed by a PAYGO rule, which means that you can't increase spending or cut taxes without providing for it.

But in fact, in the last several months we have increased the projected debt accumulation by over $1.5 trillion in the next 10 years because of decisions that this institution made to both cut taxes and increase spending.

So I guess that could be characterized as dishonest in light of the arguments being advanced today. But I would prefer to render it less personal and just suggest it is not, frankly, terribly consistent, Mr. Chairman.

And with that, I yield back the balance of my time.

Chairman DUFFY. The gentleman yields back.

The Chair now recognizes the gentlelady from Missouri, Mrs. Wagner, for 5 minutes.

Mrs. WAGNER. Thank you, Mr. Chairman.

And thank you to our esteemed panel for coming before this subcommittee to discuss this important issue of our Nation's debt, which now stands at an outrageous $19 trillion.

For Congress, the debt ceiling should be an important and necessary tool to look back on our spending policies in order to find ways to cut this massive Federal Government. Instead, this Administration has used the debt ceiling as simply a blank check and a political attack vehicle.

The American people are tired of the dysfunction in Washington and tired of their elected officials and leaders failing to get things done, and cutting our out-of-control and irresponsible debt is something the American people want done.

In 2013, when I and a number of my House colleagues had the privilege of going to the White House to negotiate in very good faith with the President on the debt ceiling, he decided to use the opportunity to lecture and pontificate, not negotiate. And I was there.

He used dramatic rhetoric such as not wanting to, "negotiate with a gun pointed at their heads," and used the press then to paint House Republicans as unwilling to talk and address the peoples' concern about our fiscally, as you all have stated, unsustainable and, I think as a mother of three, immoral debt.

Now with these new revelations, and frankly, that is what we are here to discuss, Mr. Chairman, these revelations produced by this committee, it is clear that the Administration manufactured and hyped up the crisis in order to prevent, I think, Republicans

and Congress, who are committed to slashing our debt, from enact-
ing smart and responsible fiscal policy.

Knowing now that the Administration was capable of prioritizing
debt payments and actually running tabletop exercises after reaching the debt limit, do you find the Administration's statements to
the contrary disingenuous, Ms. de Rugy?

Ms. DE RUGY. It is politics, so I guess I am not surprised.

Mrs. WAGNER. I think it is politics, too. So you do believe that
the Administration had political motivations for making these misleading statements?

Ms. DE RUGY. I think the document makes it pretty clear. But
one other thing that is also important is to actually not lose sight
of why we are talking about prioritization, right? Why do you want
to prioritize payments? So all of you can actually find a way out
of the debt mess, especially the explosion going forward that we are
talking about.

So it is not just like not paying some of our obligations just for
the sake of not paying some of our obligations. The ideas is a productive process that will lead to fundamental reform, an agreement
among you to actually lead to a compromise to finding a way out
of, honestly, putting a gigantic burden on our children.

Mrs. WAGNER. I agree.

And Ms. Boccia, shouldn't the public and Congress have the right
to know that the Administration has made these "contingency"
plans?

Ms. BOCCIA. I think that the debt limit presents a game of chick-
en in which it is in the Executive Branch's interest not to reveal
key information, like this committee just revealed yesterday, in
order to leverage this to force Congress into just raising the debt
limit, which Congress has complied with numerous times.

I am very concerned that in fact we do not have a debt limit at
this point. We have a debt limit suspension. There is no limit on
borrowing.

Mrs. WAGNER. It is a blank check.

Ms. BOCCIA. That is right.

Mrs. WAGNER. And it is outrageous and it is immoral as far as
I am concerned.

Ms. Boccia, I hope I am pronouncing that correctly, did the Administration's choice to, I believe, play politics by withholding information about the Administration's ability to make payments on the
debt create unnecessary uncertainty in the markets?

Ms. BOCCIA. Because Congress hasn't been able to give guidance
to the Administration on how to act at the debt limit, the Administration does have the leverage to refuse to pay our debt obligations.
And putting that risk out there to use as political leverage, I think
is very dangerous, because it reduces investor confidence.

However, we had numerous rating agencies, in particularly
Moody's and Fitch, say they did expect the Treasury to honor its
obligations to the United States' debt holders.

Mrs. WAGNER. And quickly in my time that is left, Dr. Mitchell,
oftentimes we see yields on short-term Treasuries spike during
these debt ceiling negotiations, which increases the cost of borrowing for the Federal Government. Is it possible that Treasury's

decision to withhold information on making debt prioritization payments end up costing the government more money?

Mr. MITCHELL. If you look at the GAO report from July 2015,
they estimate that tens of millions of dollars of additional interests
costs resulted from the Administration's lack of forthcomingness,
honesty.

Mrs. WAGNER. Tens of millions of dollars because this Administration told me, and I was there, this President said he wouldn't
negotiate when we had a gun to their heads, and he cost this country and the taxpayers and the people tens of millions of dollars.

I thank you.

I yield back. And I appreciate your indulgence.

Chairman DUFFY. The gentlelady yields back time she does not
have.

[laughter]

The Chair now recognizes the gentleman from Colorado, Mr. Tipton, for 5 minutes.

Mr. TIPTON. Thank you, Mr. Chairman.

And I thank our panel for taking the time to be here.

Ms. Boccia, you just mentioned a game of chicken that the Administration was playing. Did that impact our markets?

Ms. BOCCIA. If we look at the GAO report, then yes. If investors
have no confidence that the Administration will do what is right
and what is in the best interests of the United States, which would
be to prioritize interest and principal on the debt during a debt
limit impasse, then investors may demand higher interest rates or
refuse to buy bonds during certain periods if they are not sure that
they will be repaid.

Mr. TIPTON. So that did hurt the United States. Do you find it
irresponsible of Secretary Lew to have made comments to Congress
that we simply cannot pay the interest, pay the principal and the
interest, be able to service portions of the debt, while at the same
time they were making plans to do that very thing? Do they hold
some culpability in roiling those markets?

Ms. BOCCIA. I am glad to hear that the Treasury was responsible
enough to make contingency plans, even though they indicated otherwise to the public. I would like for government to be honest, both
to Congress and to the American public. It doesn't always happen
for political reasons.

Mr. TIPTON. So that probably ties back to Dr. Stone's comments
that candidate Obama rather than President Obama was being
reckless when he had talked about the debt ceiling and then was
concurrently reckless as President of the United States by instructing his Treasury Secretary to not be forthcoming with the American people. Is that accurate?

Mr. STONE. I didn't say the second.

Mr. TIPTON. But it is accurate.

Mr. STONE. No, it is not accurate. It is one thing when politicians
are grandstanding over the debt limit. I am not defending the
Treasury on whether they hid information or not. I am not com-
menting on that.

But the Treasury was very forthcoming about all of the steps it
was going to take after you hit the debt limit to try to arrange payments and things, to try to prevent a default.

Mr. TIPTON. I think we can probably dispute that from that report that they were holding that back.

But you know, we were raising hands here. Who on the panel
thinks that we can continue as a Nation to spend more than we
take in? Let the record show no one thinks that we can continue
to spend more than we are taking in as a country.

When we were looking at—Dr. Stone thinks we can spend more
than we take in.

Mr. STONE. We can't spend a lot more than we take in. But in
dollar terms, if we stabilize the debt—

Mr. TIPTON. How well did that work out for Greece, Dr. Stone?

Mr. STONE. Greece is a completely different example.

Mr. TIPTON. It's a completely different example?

Mr. STONE. Greece cannot borrow in its own currency. Greece
cannot—

Mr. TIPTON. No, I think we have probably—Ms. Boccia, you had
mentioned in your testimony that in the 2015 International Monetary Fund working paper, they concluded that a high level of public
debt accompanied with consistent growth in that debt is a problem.
Why is that going to be a continuing problem? Dr. Stone doesn't
seem to think so.

Ms. BOCCIA. We are seeing increasing evidence from economists
across a wide range of spectrum, even those set out to counter the
notion that high public debt hurts economic growth, they are not
able to refute that.

High public debt does hurt growth, but I think one of the main
reasons for that is because it is fueled by greater spending. We
don't have a tax problem. Taxes are at their historical level and rising above. What we have is a spending problem.

I think Congress also needs to play its part. And the congressional budget takes many steps in the right direction, but Congress
still has not put forth implementing legislation to truly balance the
budget.

Mr. TIPTON. And I appreciate both your and Dr. de Rugy's comments of the hand-in-glove, of spending versus the debt that we
have. We need to be able to address both of those.

But Dr. Mitchell, could you maybe tell us what signals we are
sending to the market by continually increasing the debt ceiling
without engaging in actually having fiscal discipline? What are we
telling the markets?

Mr. MITCHELL. It is ultimately a matter of trust whether or not
investors will get paid back. And as Dr. Stone mentioned, Japan
is still borrowing at 200 percent of GDP. We are borrowing right
now at very low rates of interest, so we are trusted. As a matter
of fact, you could maybe make an argument that we are too trusted, that markets are too trusting of government. Because if you go
back 10 years, Greece was borrowing at very low rates.

Mr. TIPTON. Just to get in, before we run out of time here, as
someone who is wanting to be paid back, when you are seeing .07
percent GDP growth in this country, are you starting to get a little
concerned that you are going to be paid back?

Mr. MITCHELL. I am very concerned that with a long-term future
of government growing faster than the private sector, we are on a
path to becoming Greece if we don't engage in structural reform.

Mr. TIPTON. Thank you, sir.

I yield back.

Chairman DUFFY. The gentleman yields back.

The Chair now recognizes the gentleman from Maine, Mr. Poliquin, for 5 minutes.

Mr. POLIQUIN. Thank you, Mr. Chairman; I appreciate it very much.

And thank you all for being here today.

Before I entered Congress a year ago, I was the State treasurer in Maine and a small-business owner. I still am a small-business owner. And one of the things that we learned, those of us who are business owners is: number one, live within your means; and number two, be very, very careful with debt.

Now, I will tell you, one of the things that we learned, Mr. Chairman, back in Maine when I was State treasurer, we actually had a debt clock that was unwinding. I come in here every hearing and I look at that $19 trillion continuing to spool up and it makes me sick to my stomach. It makes me sick to my stomach because there aren't enough people, frankly, on the other side of the aisle who have the guts to deal with this. They talk about it, but all they want is bigger government, more spending, and more debt, which results in higher taxes. And they, of course, want more regulations and higher energy costs, and that kills jobs.

And it kills jobs, that is important, because if our folks don't have jobs, then they don't pay taxes, they are more dependent on the government, and we don't have the cash flow to meet our obligations.

Now, the reason we were able to unwind our debt clock in Maine during 2011, 2012 is because we attacked a fundamental issue dealing with the debt, which is our unfunded pension liability, public pension fund. We looked it in the eye, we were serious about it, we engaged all stakeholders and we reduced 41 percent of that pension debt, which caused the debt clock to unwind.

Now, we have the same problem here, Mr. Chairman. We have a $15 trillion unfunded defined benefit pension plan called Social Security. Now, we all know in this room and the folks who are listening, two-thirds of our budget is on autopilot in four programs: Medicare; Medicaid; Social Security; and interest on the debt, which isn't a program, but it continues to grow.

When are we going to have a serious conversation with the kids in this country, 25- and 30-year-old folks to say, if you want these programs that are growing a lot faster than our tax revenues, we need to make some changes? We know what to do; it is simple math.

Now, I am not talking about our seniors, Mr. Chairman, who have paid into these programs their whole lives and are depending on these programs. No change for them. But we have millennials, and there are a lot of them, a lot more than the baby boomers, and we can fix this.

So that is one of the reasons, Mr. Chairman, why I support, and I know you do, too, and those on this side of the aisle do, a balanced budget amendment of the Constitution. My second day here, when I was still trying to find out where the men's room was. I co-sponsored that bill. I think it would be the greatest institutional tool that Washington could have. Force Washington to live within its means so we can start paying down our debt.

Now, Mr. Chairman, when we have Mr. Lew coming in here, the Secretary of the Treasury, telling us, well, the debt is no big deal, it is only 3, 4 percent of the GDP, we have talked about it today, you have, Mr. Chairman, thank you, the interest payments on that debt are now twice what we spend on veterans' benefits in a year. They are projected to exceed what we spend to defend our country in 8 years. It is a big deal.

Now, I would say also, Mr. Chairman, that 4 years ago the annual budget deficit was $1.3 trillion, and it is now $440 billion. We have a long way to go, but it has been cut in two-thirds, not because some folks don't want to spend more, but because Republicans are trying to be fiscally disciplined and have spending caps in place.

So my question to you, Mr. Mitchell, is—you have been around this town a lot longer than I have—do you think we have enough people in Congress who have the guts to address our spending problem, who will allow us to start whittling away at that $19 trillion debt that is chewing up our budget and putting a yoke around our kids' necks, that they are going to be saddled with, that creates a tremendous dark cloud above our economy and kills jobs and kills the kids of our future? What do you think?

Mr. MITCHELL. Normally, I am a pessimist, but for 5 years in a row the House has voted for a budget resolution that is based on the assumption of some genuine and serious reform to slow the growth of entitlement spending.

And the Senate even did something sort of like that last year. So I think there is a recognition, to some degree, that there is a very serious problem.

Obviously, those moves in Congress couldn't go anywhere because of opposition from the White House. But maybe, just maybe, within a couple of years we will be able to take a serious step in terms of preventing America from become Greece.

Mr. MITCHELL. Thank you very much, Mr. Mitchell.

Dr. Stone, what do you think? Do you think we have enough people in Congress on both sides of the aisle? I know we do on this side. Do you think we have enough on the Democrats' side who are fiscally disciplined and conservative enough to start getting their act together and start living within our means? What do you think, sir?

Mr. STONE. I think that in 2011 when we had the debt ceiling crisis and we had a commission, we had a super committee in Congress to try to make decisions. It was a bipartisan failure to come up with a permanent solution. It is hard choices. It takes—

Mr. POLIQUIN. We don't need a commission, Mr. Stone, to make a decision, but we know what to do.

Mr. STONE. No, no, no, no, no.

Mr. POLIQUIN. This is all about politics and simple math.

Mr. STONE. No, I am not talking about a commission. I was talking about a committee of Congress, a super committee.

Chairman DUFFY. The gentleman's time has expired.

Mr. Stone, the gentleman's time has expired.

Mr. POLIQUIN. Thank you very much, Mr. Chairman. I yield back my time which I don't have.

Chairman DUFFY. Thank you, you do not have any.

The Chair now recognizes the gentleman from Arkansas, Mr. Hill, for 5 minutes.

Mr. HILL. Thank you, Mr. Chairman.

And I thank the panel for being with us. It's good to see my old friend, Dan Mitchell.

I am reminded by listening to this discussion, and from my friend Mr. Heck, as a 30-year banker and business guy, of the woman who comes into the bank branch and says, "I can't be overdrawn in my account." And the bank manager says, "But you are." And she says, "I can't be; I still have checks."

No laughter, oh well. Banking jokes just don't go over like they used to.

[laughter]

Thank you. Thank you to the gentleman from South Carolina.

As a former Treasury official, it really saddens me to read comments from the New York Fed which say that the Treasury's position is crazy, counterproductive, and is adding risk to the system. And that my friend, former Treasury official, now a Governor of the Federal Reserve System, Jay Powell, says that Treasury is politicizing important fiscal policy.

I think we should all be shocked by that, Democrats and Republicans, because there is no room for that in the proper governance of our country. And it goes absolutely against everything Hamilton put in place back in his report on the public debt, 1790.

I am interested in some quick responses and then I have a couple of questions. Does everybody here—and I am interested because I have kind of gotten a couple of different feelings—support the fact that we have a debt limit and it comes up and we debate it? Just raise your hands if you support the existing debt limit statute, effectively. Okay, three yes and one no.

And do you all support Congressman McClintock's bill that we passed in the House last year? If you would raise your hands on that?

Ms. BOCCIA. I am not sure that I am legally allowed to do this.

Ms. DE RUGY. I was going to say, I support the policy.

Mr. HILL. Well, his bill was this issue of being able to, while we are negotiating a debt limit crisis, be able to continue to issue securities to pay the interest and keep payments current.

Do you support a Greenspan-type commission which was used in 1983 to tackle something like Medicare? Is that an idea? Or do you think, as my friend from Maine says, it should be specifically the burden of the Congress? Or do you like the idea of an independent commission that gives Congress a BRAC, up-or-down vote type approach?

Ms. DE RUGY. That is different.

Mr. HILL. You may comment on that, if you like.

Dr. Mitchell, would you like to comment on that?

Ms. DE RUGY. I can comment on this. The 1983 commission was different from a BRAC commission. And the result led to increasing taxes and a lot of other problems that we are facing right now.

Mr. HILL. Dan, any comment?

Mr. MITCHELL. As Dr. de Rugy said, the 1983 Social Security commission did lead to some significant tax increases. It did not lead to the kind of long-run structural reform that I think would have been a better approach.

I do like the idea of doing anything, including commissions, that will at least help to inform the debate. But I am just not overly happy with the results we got from that one.

Mr. HILL. Yes. I go home, and whenever I am in town hall meetings, people are so fixated on the trillion dollars, a third of the budget that we vote on and debate on here in the appropriations process. And it is just a disproportionate amount of things.

I think Members of Congress here, when they are at home and we never hear from our constituents in a detailed, thoughtful way about the two-thirds of the budget that I think has been the anchor of our conversations today, that I agree have a big demographic, structural component to them.

Dr. Stone, you talked about general thoughts about levels of debt to GDP. You are a classic economist on the one hand and on the other hand in your overview of that. But in the Reinhart/Rogoff papers that were delivered to NBER and all that back in 2008, 2009, they had specific views on debt to GDP levels for the long run.

And I would be interested in each of your views on what you think that band is of where we need to move debt to GDP to have the national debt return to being a national blessing, and thus not be excessive.

Dr. Mitchell?

Mr. MITCHELL. As I mentioned before, Japan has government debt 200 percent of GDP. They can still borrow. Argentina would probably be in default if they tried to go to 50 percent of GDP. So it really depends on the underlying conditions in the country, which is why I think the most important thing to focus on is capping the growth of government spending relative to the economy.

The Swiss debt brake does that; it has been very, very successful. Hong Kong, Article 107 of their basic law, the goal isn't to balance the budget per se, it is to make sure government doesn't grow faster than the private sector.

If we could have a rule like that where you address the underlying disease of too much government, then the symptom of red ink disappears. So I want to deal with the underlying problem. We deal with the underlying problem and the symptom of borrowing goes away.

Mr. HILL. Thank you, Mr. Chairman.

Chairman DUFFY. The gentleman's time has expired.

The Chair now recognizes the ranking member of the subcommittee, the gentleman from Texas, Mr. Green, for 5 minutes.

Mr. GREEN. Thank you, Mr. Chairman.

And I would like to simply reiterate that my friends are in the Majority. To continue to blame the Democrats makes little sense to your voting public. They expect you to produce legislation. You want a constitutional amendment? You are in the Majority. You want to pass a bill that allows prioritization? You are in the Majority. You can do it. Believe me, trust me, you are in the Majority; you don't have to depend on Democrats to get it done.

I think in the spirit of compromise that would be the better thing to do, but you are not willing to compromise. Therein lies the problem. If you want to do it, pass McClintock, pass it through the Senate, send it to the President, let us see if he will sign it. If he does not, then you go back through regular order and you produce something that we can all agree on to the extent that you have a Majority in the House, a Majority in the Senate, and a President to sign it.

But don't behave like you are in the Minority and it is the mean old Democrats who won't let you pass legislation. It never stopped you from passing a repeal of the Affordable Care Act more than 50 times, more than 50 times, and there are still other repeals of it pending. You have repealed it consistently, okay? Then act like you are in the Majority and pass your legislation.

Let us go to Mr. Stone.

Mr. Stone, there was a comment made about Greece and you did not have an opportunity to finish. There was a comparison being made. Would you kindly finish your commentary?

Mr. STONE. As I was saying, and Dr. Mitchell agrees, Japan is able to borrow with a debt ratio of 200 percent of GDP. And that is because Japan, the United States, and the U.K. borrow in their own currencies and have flexible exchange rates. That allows them to adjust.

Now, nobody here, including me, thinks that the current GDP projections are ultimately sustainable. We are discussing whether the debt limit is a worthwhile tool to try to discipline our spending.

Mr. GREEN. Exactly.

Mr. STONE. And I strongly disagree with the idea that the debt limit has much to do with it or the prioritization. The prioritization makes sure that certain bills get paid and maybe some bondholders are happy with that, but there are a lot of bills that don't get paid and that doesn't make us look like a very fiscally responsible country and it makes it look like it is okay to not pay those bills in a protracted debt negotiation.

Mr. GREEN. I appreciate your indicating that this is not an effective tool because of the consequences associated with a possible shutdown. And that causes me to harken back to 2011 and what Moody's did when they downgraded us and we didn't have the shutdown. We were downgraded. And I think that Moody's gave us a negative and S&P put us on a credit watch.

So our opinions count, but the opinions of the agencies that rate us count as well. And while we may pay P&I, it will cause a good deal of consternation in international markets as to whether or not we are going to pay all of our bills and eventually not pay P&I. Why put ourselves in that position? Why don't we legislate now, given that we have more than 400 days to do what Ms. de Rugy says, pass her recommendations if you would like to?

Don't expect me to vote for all of the things that you would support. But if we can reach some sort of compromise, I think we can get this done. The problem is that there are people who don't want to compromise; they want us to support anything and everything and leave behind a good many people who are going to suffer as a result of the crisis that we will manufacture.

To this end, it is my belief, Mr. Chairman, that Social Security is important to people who are receiving it. And I think we can sustain it. We can support it without it being a detriment to the economy. We have to work together and work out a compromise on Social Security. But we are not doing that.

Rather than do that with Social Security as well as with Medicare, we are trying to find a clever way to create a debt crisis so that we can have the Administration prioritize.

If you want a prioritizing to take place, pass the legislation, get it done. You are the Majority, it is your job to get it done. Don't whine and cry about how the Democrats won't support us and are there enough people here willing to do it. Yes, there are enough people willing to do it if you have the Majority and you use it properly.

I yield back.

Chairman DUFFY. The gentleman yields back.

The Chair now recognizes the gentleman from South Carolina, Mr. Mulvaney, for 5 minutes.

Mr. MULVANEY. Mr. Stone, in your report you cite a GAO report which says, regarding the debt ceiling crisis in 2011, "When the Treasury was close to breaching the debt limit, investors reported taking the unprecedented action of systematically avoiding certain Treasury securities. That cost from the Treasury from, roughly, $38 million to more than $70 million in higher interest costs, amounting to, in essence, nothing more than a waste of taxpayers' money." I take it that was because of the uncertainty in the markets. That is why interest rates go up, or that is one of the reasons that they do.

If the Treasury had information at that time that could have calmed the markets by letting the markets know that we would have paid principal and interest, do you think they should have revealed it?

Let me put it this way, if they had revealed it, would it have calmed the markets?

Mr. STONE. It may have calmed the markets, but it wouldn't have—it may have partially calmed the markets because—

Mr. MULVANEY. Do you think that the guys and gals who were thinking about buying Treasuries were worried about whether or not the national parks were going to be open? Or do you think they were worried about getting their money back if they bought Treasuries?

Mr. STONE. They were worried about getting their money back.

Mr. MULVANEY. And if the Treasury had information that would have assured them they would have gotten their money back, we might have saved that $38 million to $70 million, might we not? Mr.

STONE. We might not have seen that shifting away from certain securities, given the timing of it.

Mr. MULVANEY. You mention in your testimony in another place, your written testimony, it says that the debt ceiling, "plays no constructive role in enforcing budget discipline; rather, it encourages reckless brinkmanship." You have mentioned that a couple of times in your testimony.

Would you be surprised that according to AEI, in 1979 the debt ceiling debate was used in order to leverage and require the President to present balanced budgets in the next following years, which he did? In 1980, the debt ceiling debate was used to reform import tariffs. In 1985, the debt ceiling was used to reform cigarette taxes and the alternative minimum tax.

And there are several folks who were here in the 1990s who will swear to you that the debt ceiling discussion during the 1990s led directly to the balanced budgets later that decade.

So do you still stand by your testimony that it is never used in order to reach compromise that speaks to fiscal matters?

Mr. STONE. No, I didn't say it was never used to reach compromise, although—

Mr. MULVANEY. It says it plays no constructive role. Did it play a constructive role in 1979, 1980, 1985, and the 1990s?

Mr. STONE. As a bargaining chip, I don't view that. I view the risks much too high relative to any—

Mr. MULVANEY. That is not what you said. You said it plays no constructive role. But you would have to admit that in those circumstances, which I found in 3 minutes on the Internet, they were used for constructive purposes.

Mr. STONE. I will use a dramatic analogy. If you play Russian roulette and you pull a blank—

Mr. MULVANEY. Okay. So your testimony is hyperbole then and not really—

Mr. STONE. No, no.

Mr. MULVANEY. Okay, all right, that is fine.

Last issue, default. Let us define default because it used to mean not paying interest on our debt or paying our principal on our debt. In fact, if you go back and you watch Secretary Lew's testimony, I have been doing this now since 2011, as has Mr. Duffy, we were on Joint Economic together, it used to be that we wouldn't be able to pay our financial obligations, we wouldn't be able to pay principal and interest. That changed and now the Administration uses the same terminology you use, which is we wouldn't be able to pay our obligations, making the equivalent that all payments are the same.

So let us explore that a little bit. By the way, do we have a contractual obligation to pay back the debt? When we sell a Treasury to Mr. Duffy, are we making a legal promise to pay him back? Dr. Stone?

Mr. STONE. Is the principal going to be repaid? Yes.

Mr. MULVANEY. Yes, it is a legally enforceable promise to pay, right?

Mr. STONE. Yes.

Mr. MULVANEY. Let's see, last year, a couple of years ago, we spent $3 million on a NASA study on how Congress works. Does that rise to the same level of obligation, in your mind, as the promise to pay Mr. Duffy back the money with which he has bought a Treasury?

Mr. STONE. We have obligations to honor all of our—we are required under the Constitution to honor all of our obligations. There is a conflict.

Mr. MULVANEY. Okay. I am trying to drill down into that, Dr. Stone, because we are using the English language. It may be different at Swarthmore than it was at Georgetown, but I am just trying to figure out where we are. Is the obligation that we pay, for lack of a better word, NASA $3 million to study Congress—by the way, I could get a lot more fun on a list. We spent a couple hundred thousand dollars on studying the effect of cocaine on the sex habits of Japanese quail. If you would rather me use that example, I could, but let us stay with NASA for a second.

Does the obligation that we have to pay NASA to study us rise to the same level legally as the obligation to pay Mr. Duffy back the money he lent us by buying a Treasury?

Mr. STONE. I think you are not asking legally, you are asking in a sense of—

Mr. MULVANEY. Well, pick one. Pick a legal sense, pick a political sense, are they of the same import, in your mind?

Mr. STONE. Would the harm of not paying our financial obligations compare with a tiny amount of a study? No.

Mr. MULVANEY. Okay.

Mr. STONE. But for doctors, for hospitals—

Mr. MULVANEY. And in principle, we are not breaking new ground here, Dr. Stone. I think everybody admits that some of the obligations of the Federal Government are more important than others. It is not going against some liberal/progressive orthodoxy to say it is more important to pay the debt than it is to pay to study quails having sex. That shouldn't be outrageous. If it is, we have a lot bigger issue to deal with.

So I think you see what I am getting at, which is we are going to prioritize at some point. We do all the time. We admit to ourselves that the debt is more important than paying to study Congress or paying to study quails having sex. And that is all that we are asking to do in the prioritization bill.

Mr. STONE. You prioritize when you pass a budget and pass laws for appropriations.

Mr. MULVANEY. Can NASA sue us?

Mr. STONE. And when the bills come due, you pay them.

Mr. MULVANEY. Can NASA sue us to get the money? Mr. Duffy can sue us to get the money, can NASA sue us to get the money? We all know the answer to that.

I wish we had more time to do this. This is the third or fourth time you and I have done this the last couple of years. I always enjoy your participation.

Mr. STONE. It was fun.

[laughter]

Mr. MULVANEY. I look forward to having you back. Thanks, Dr. Stone.

Chairman DUFFY. The gentleman yields back. Thank you for your common-sense questions.

The Chair notes that some Members may have additional questions for this panel, which they may wish to submit in writing. Without objection, the hearing record will remain open for 5 legislative days for Members to submit written questions to these witnesses and to place their responses in the record. Also, without objection, Members will have 5 legislative days to submit extraneous materials to the Chair for inclusion in the record.

I appreciate your time and your insight into today's hearing.

And so without objection, this hearing is now adjourned.

[Whereupon, at 4:28 p.m., the hearing was adjourned.]

APPENDIX

February 2, 2016

214 Massachusetts Avenue, NE • Washington DC 20002 • (202) 546-4400 • heritage.org

CONGRESSIONAL TESTIMONY

The Debt Limit: A Key Action-Forcing Tool to Control Spending and the Debt

**Testimony before
The Committee on Financial Services
Subcommittee on Oversight and
Investigations
United States House**

February 2, 2016

**Romina Boccia
Grover M. Hermann Research Fellow in Federal
Budgetary Affairs and Deputy Director, Roe Institute
The Heritage Foundation**

Chairman Sean P. Duffy, Ranking Member Alan Green, Members of the House Financial Services Subcommittee on Oversight and Investigations, thank you for the opportunity to testify today. My name is Romina Boccia. I am the Grover M. Hermann Research Fellow in Federal Budgetary Affairs and Deputy Director in the Thomas A. Roe Institute for Economic Policy Studies at The Heritage Foundation. The views I express in this testimony are my own, and should not be construed as representing any official position of The Heritage Foundation.

The nation is on a fiscal collision course. Absent presidential and congressional leadership through the regular budget process, the debt limit is a key action-forcing tool that drives attention toward the nation's precarious fiscal state, and enables lawmakers to leverage a crisis scenario for necessary and urgent policy reforms that might not otherwise come about.

Though the debt limit is a blunt tool to motivate fiscal discipline, a brief self-imposed fiscal crisis to enact structural policy reforms that rein in growing spending and debt may very well be the lesser evil. This is especially true in comparison with an unexpected, sudden, and drastic fiscal crisis that leaves policymakers with few tools to respond in a predictable and gradual manner. Desperate times require desperate measures.

Our Nation's Fiscal Condition

The latest fiscal and economic projections by the Congressional Budget Office (CBO), published in its January 2015 *Budget and Economic Outlook,*[1] paint a clear picture. Spending and debt are growing at an unsustainable pace; greatly increasing the risks of a sudden fiscal crisis during which investors would demand much higher interest rates to continue lending to the U.S. government.

The CBO projects that outlays will grow from $3.7 trillion in 2015 to $6.4 trillion in 2026, in nominal dollar terms. Moreover, spending growth is projected to outpace economic growth, as outlays are expected to grow from 20.7 percent of gross domestic product (GDP) in 2015 to 23.1 percent of GDP in 2026. Meanwhile, tax revenues are projected to remain relatively stable at around 18 percent of GDP. Growing spending is clearly the culprit responsible for growing deficits and debt.

The annual deficit is growing again, after a short respite brought about by an economy recovering from the Great Recession, rising tax revenues, lower spending on automatic stabilizers, and the spending caps imposed by the Budget Control Act of 2011. The CBO now projects that deficits will reach annual trillion dollar levels as soon as 2022, growing to nearly $1.4 trillion by 2026. Cumulative deficits are now projected at $9.4 trillion just over the next decade.

---

[1] Congressional Budget Office, *The Budget and Economic Outlook: 2016 to 2026*, January 25, 2015, https://www.cbo.gov/publication/51129 (accessed January 28, 2016).

Growing spending is driving debt to economically harmful levels. Projected deficits would push debt held by the public to 86 percent of GDP by the end of the decade, or nearly twice the historical average level.

Debt Drags Down Growth

Several economists, employing different methods, have arrived at the same conclusion: high levels of public debt are correlated with lower levels of economic growth. While there is no definite threshold, public debt levels at, or nearing, the size of an industrialized country's economy are more robustly correlated with lower levels of growth. A 2013 literature review by my Heritage colleague, Dr. Salim Furth, covered research by three different teams of economists, all of which separately showed that high government debt has a negative effect on long-term economic growth. "When government debt grows, private investment shrinks, lowering future growth and future wages," concludes Furth.[2]

Since then, even more research has surfaced drawing a close link between depressed economic growth in the face of high public debt levels.

Afonso and Alves, in a 2014 paper titled "The Role of Government Debt in Economic Growth," reviewed data for 14 European countries from 1970 to 2012. The authors identify a clear negative link between high public debt and economic growth. Servicing the interest on the public debt has the most harmful effects. According to the authors, "we can conclude that, as is usually affirmed, debt is negative for growth, both in the short and long-term…. When we analyse both debt-to-GDP ratio and debt service variables, the latter has a much more negative effect on economic performance when compared with debt."[3]

A 2015 International Monetary Fund (IMF) working paper by Alexander Chudik, Kamiar Mohaddes, M. Hashem Pesaran, and Mehdi Raissi studies whether there is a definitive threshold at which debt begins to hurt growth and whether there is a causal link between high debt and slow economic growth. While the authors reject the hypothesis that high public debt levels always slow growth, they find a statistically significant threshold effect for countries whose debt levels are not only high, but growing. The authors stress the importance of which direction the debt is heading.

Because debt perceptions are dependent on expectations by investors and the public, debt growth or shrinkage sends powerful signals beyond what is conveyed by threshold levels. Debt trajectory matters. According to the authors, "regardless of the threshold, however, we find significant negative long-run effects of public debt build-up on output growth."[4]

---

[2]Salim Furth, "High Debt Is a Real Drag," Heritage Foundation *Issue Brief* No. 3859, February 22, 2013, http://www.heritage.org/research/reports/2013/02/how-a-high-national-debt-impacts-the-economy.

[3]Antonio Afonso and Jose Alves, "The Role of Government Debt in Economic Growth," working paper, Social Science Research Network, 2014.

[4]Alexaner Chudik, Kamiar Mohaddes, M. Hashem Pesaran, and Mehdi Raissi, "Is There a Debt-threshold Effect on Output Growth?" 2015, https://www.imf.org/external/pubs/cat/longres.aspx?sk=43260.0 (accessed January 28, 2016).

Even those analysts who sought to intentionally reject the thesis, that high debt causes growth to slow, were unable to rule out economic drag from high levels of public debt. Ugo Panizza and Andrea F Presbitero set out to do just that in a 2012 paper. The authors concluded that the "fact that we do not find a negative effect of debt on growth does not mean that countries can sustain any level of debt. There is clearly a level of debt beyond which debt becomes unsustainable, and a debt-to-GDP ratio at which debt overhang, with all its distortionary effects, kicks in."[5]

How does high public debt negatively impact long-term growth prospects? Through which mechanisms do high public debt levels exert downward pressure on the economy?

Deficit-spending allows government to consume resources today at a cost to future generations. This enables greater government spending than would be the case if the government had to raise all of the revenue to finance its spending in the current period. Raising taxes is more politically difficult than is increasing deficits. By shifting some of the burden of today's government spending to younger generations, government is able to consume more of the economy's resources than it otherwise could.

Without a tight budget constraint to impose spending discipline, government spending is also less likely to go toward financing the highest priority projects. More of the spending will go to frivolous projects that benefit well-connected interested groups, instead of the public interest, and federal agencies are better able to sustain mismanagement and waste. This wastes economic resources that could have been put to better use in the private sector.

High public debt levels demand high debt service costs. Federal spending on interest payments draws on dollars that could have otherwise been spent on current national priorities, instead of servicing the sins of the past. Every dollar that goes toward interest spending is a dollar that is no longer available for national defense, infrastructure, and other public services.

Investor concerns about the sustainability of large and growing public debt may demand higher interest rates to continue lending to the government. Spending pressures could put pressure on tax revenues, motivating lawmakers to raise taxes, which harms private spending and investment. In the absence of greater revenue, government may resort to devaluation of the dollar to lower the public debt burden.

The CBO in its most recent *Long-Term Outlook* also emphasized reduced flexibility to respond to challenges in the event of an economic or fiscal crisis. According to the CBO:

> The large amount of debt would restrict policymakers' ability to use tax and spending policies to respond to unexpected challenges, such as economic downturns or financial crises. As a result, those challenges would tend to have

---

[5]Uga Panizza and Andrea F. Presbitero, "Is High Public Debt Harmful for Economic Growth?" Vox, April 22, 2012, http://www.voxeu.org/article/high-public-debt-harmful-economic-growth-new-evidence (accessed January 28, 2016).

larger negative effects on the economy and on people's well-being than they would otherwise. The large amount of debt could also compromise national security by constraining defense spending in times of international crisis or by limiting the country's ability to prepare for such a crisis.[6]

Why the Debt Limit Matters

Congress has several legislative tools to address the drivers of growing spending and debt. Importantly, Congress's budget resolution affords lawmakers not only a forum to lay out its action plan to return the budget to balance; it also provides a fast-track legislative process to implement reforms that control government spending programs. However, this process, called reconciliation, requires active engagement by Congress. If Congress fails to make use of reconciliation, lawmakers face no immediate consequences as debt and spending continue spiraling out of control.

The debt limit, on the other hand, does provide an urgent and important deadline, enforced by painful fiscal measures, to motivate Congress to take action. At the same time, the debt limit provides the political cover necessary to make unpopular, but necessary, legislative decisions. Reducing entitlement benefits is a prime example.

The debt limit is a separate check on borrowing. It limits the amount of money or the dates during which the Treasury is authorized to borrow to finance federal deficit spending. At the debt limit, Treasury finds itself unable to meet all federal payment obligations as they come due. Absent specific guidance by Congress, Treasury and the President are confronted with a difficult decision: prioritize spending in accordance with the national interest (making judgments that will be closely scrutinized in courts and by the public), or delay payments across the board, paying bills in the order in which they come due when sufficient revenues are available, regardless of the nature of those bills.

Several analysts and pundits argue that the debt limit is an archaic construct that serves no useful purpose. They argue that because Congress authorizes all spending, it does not make sense to have a separate limit on borrowing. As one proponent of repealing the debt limit put it: "members are only covering their tracks for supporting more spending and big tax giveaways.... Very simply, they have voted to spend the money, but they don't want to pay the bill."[7]

Ideally, congressional decisions to spend and borrow would be aligned. However, there are at least three reasons why the debt limit serves a useful purpose: (1) the programs driving the majority of the growth in federal spending were authorized decades ago and are allowed to grow on autopilot with few congressional action-forcing deadlines to change those programs' trajectories; (2) the public does not recognize that it is their most cherished entitlement programs that are driving the growth in spending and the debt and

---

[6]Congressional Budget Office, *The 2015 Long-Term Budget Outlook*, 2015, https://www.cbo.gov/publication/50250 (accessed January 18, 2016).

[7]Scott Lilly, "Congress Shouldn't Raise the 'Debt Limit'—It Should Repeal It," Center For American Progress, October 15, 2013.

the debt limit debate can help to elevate public understanding while at the same time providing political cover for lawmakers who seek to reduce spending on those programs; and (3) lawmakers only control some of the factors that drive the growth in the debt, and economic downturns or unanticipated increases in interest costs may mean that previously authorized spending should be reconsidered in light of factors outside Congress's control.

Autopilot Spending

The federal budget is separated into three major categories: discretionary spending, mandatory spending, and net interest. The key difference between mandatory and discretionary spending is that discretionary spending receives its source of funding from annual appropriations (some programs less frequently), while mandatory spending is governed by laws that contain the source of funding. The vast majority of mandatory spending occurs in two programs: Social Security and Medicare.

Overall, mandatory spending made up 62 percent of the budget in fiscal year 2015, and consumed nearly 13 percent of GDP.[8] Congress only appropriates about one-third of federal spending in any given year. The vast majority of federal spending grows on autopilot based on conditions put into law many Congresses ago.

In an interview on his recent book, *Dead Men Ruling*, Eugene Steuerle explained this predicament as follows:

> Today's government is constructed and constricted by programs and policies that were designed by men (women, too, but they were largely excluded) decades ago, many of whom are not with us today. Many of these programs were well designed to improve the economic and social welfare of Americans at the time they were created and some years into the future. But the world has moved on, and these programs have not.... My intention with the book was to convince the reader that this is a very different problem from a more traditional "deficit" problem that would arise when government becomes profligate through new legislation year after year. The profligacy is now built in. The former problem could often be solved by temporary legislative inaction; the new problem requires legislative action to remove it.[9]

The debt limit provides an action-forcing deadline to pursue the legislative steps necessary to rein in out-of-control autopilot spending. The debt limit can draw attention to the key drivers of spending and debt and highlight the budget reforms necessary to control the growth in debt. It can also provide political leverage to pursue those changes in laws that are necessary to change the debt trajectory.

---

[8] Congressional Budget Office, *The Budget and Economic Outlook: 2016 to 2026.*
[9] Rebecca Rolfes, "Debts of the Past Limit the Future: An Interview with Eugene Steuerle," The Gail Fosler Group, March 11, 2014, http://www.gailfosler.com/debts-past-limit-future-interview-eugene-steuerle (accessed January 28, 2016).

Political Cover

The very programs that are most responsible for the growth in spending and debt are also the most popular with voters. A Roper Center analysis at Cornell University concerning public opinion polling on questions of government spending, deficits, and debt concluded that "questions about cutting spending on government programs in the abstract tend to overstate the public's willingness to see particular programs cut."[10]

Different opinion polls tend to arrive at the same result. Americans are much more willing to support spending cuts in the abstract than they are to support spending cuts in particular programs. The only exception appears to be foreign aid.[11] The public is particularly unwilling to support cuts in Social Security and Medicare to reduce the deficit.[12] To the contrary, there is widespread support for cutting fraud, waste, and abuse. Basically anything that appears as though cutting it would have no impact on recipients of public services in the U.S. is ripe for the cutting board. If there was a painless way to balance the budget, Americans would be all for it.[13]

The false perception by the public that reductions to fraud, waste, abuse and foreign aid are sufficient to reduce government spending and control the debt creates political difficulties for lawmakers who seek to represent their constituents' wishes even if they create vast challenges for public finances and the economy. When more than half of the projected growth in federal spending over the next decade is driven by Social Security and federal health care programs—in particular Medicare, Medicaid (especially its expansion under Obamacare), and Obamacare's premium subsidies—it becomes nearly impossible to balance the budget without entitlement reform. According to the CBO, "almost half of the projected $2.5 trillion increase in total outlays from 2016 to 2026 is for Social Security and Medicare." CBO also projects that Social Security and Medicare will grow in real terms by 0.9 percentage points of GDP and 0.8 percentage points of GDP, respectively, just over the next decade.[14]

A debt limit that binds creates consequences sufficiently severe to provide political cover for lawmakers who will lead on making the important reforms that are in the long-term interest of their constituents and the nation writ large, even if their constituents do not see it that way. Presidential leadership is one key ingredient. In the same way in which

[10]Roper Center, "In the Balance: The Public, the Budget and the Deficit," Cornell.edu, January 29, 2015, http://ropercenter.cornell.edu/in-the-balance-the-public-the-budget-and-the-deficit/ (accessed January 28, 2016).

[11]Pew Research Center, "As Sequester Deadline Looms, Little Support for Cutting Most Programs," February 22, 2013, http://www.people-press.org/2013/02/22/as-sequester-deadline-looms-little-support-for-cutting-most-programs/ (accessed January 28, 2016).

[12]Pew Research Center, "Public Still Unwilling to Cut Entitlement Benefits to Reduce Deficit," April 10, 2013, http://www.pewresearch.org/daily-number/public-still-unwilling-to-cut-entitlement-benefits-to-reduce-deficit/ (accessed January 28, 2016).

[13]Michael Tanner, "This Is Going to Hurt: There Is No Painless Way to Balance the Budget," *National Review*, April 6, 2011, http://www.nationalreview.com/article/263972/going-hurt-michael-tanner (accessed January 28, 2016).

[14]Congressional Budget Office, *The Budget and Economic Outlook: 2016 to 2026.*

Congress and President Obama explained to their constituents why the Budget Control Act's spending reductions were necessary following the debt limit standoff in 2011,[15] lawmakers and the executive can justify reductions in entitlement benefits to serve the broader public interest of controlling the growth in spending and the debt, leveraging the debt limit for political cover. "Our hands were tied!"

Factors Outside Congress's Control

There are several factors that influence the size and direction of public debt. These include congressional budget decisions, the state of the economy, and interest rates. Spending and revenue decisions are factors within Congress's control. Yet, actual revenue levels are highly dependent on the state of the economy. During an economic downturn, revenue tends to fall steeply as businesses sell fewer goods and services, workers lose employment, and entities go out of business. Interest costs, likewise, represent a factor mostly outside Congress's control. If investors demanded higher interest rates as a risk premium when government borrowing seems to spiral out of control, this can suddenly raise the cost of federal borrowing.

After congressional budget decisions are made, the debt limit confronts Congress with the state of the debt. If factors outside Congress's control significantly affected the trajectory of the debt, it may be prudent to reconsider prior spending decisions to improve the fiscal situation. This does not mean that Congress should renege on obligations that are due; rather, Congress should adjust commitments going forward and the debt limit provides a legislative opportunity to make adjustments as necessary.

Prioritization

As the federal government approaches the debt limit and absent congressional action to increase the limit, Treasury does not necessarily default on debt obligations. Even while cash-strapped, the Treasury can reasonably be expected to prioritize principal and interest payments on the national debt, protecting the full faith and credit of the United States above all other spending. It is almost impossible to conceive that the Treasury and the President would choose to default on debt obligations. Doing so would have damaging economic consequences.

Treasury did employ the threat of default numerous times. Treasury argued publicly that it lacked the logistical means and the statutory authority to prioritize payments—including debt obligations—in the event of a debt limit impasse. In response to an inquiry by Senator Orrin Hatch (R–UT) in 2011 as to contingency plans Treasury may have made for a possible debt limit impasse, Treasury stated that "organizationally they viewed the option of delaying payments as the least harmful among the options under review." This interpretation of executive authority directly contradicts a previous statement by the Government Accountability Office, which asserted that Treasury has the discretion to

---

[15]Barack Obama, "Statement by the President," The White House, August 2, 2011, https://www.whitehouse.gov/the-press-office/2011/08/02/statement-president (accessed January 28, 2016).

prioritize payments:

> We are aware of no statute or any other basis for concluding that Treasury is required to pay outstanding obligations in the order in which they are presented for payment unless it chooses to do so. Treasury is free to liquidate obligations in any order it finds will best serve the interests of the United States.[16]

Treasury's assertion was likely employed to apply pressure to congressional Republicans to raise the debt limit. An Administration official, speaking on the basis of anonymity, confirmed as much, stating in 2011 that Treasury intended to prioritize meeting its debt obligations to avoid default.[17] Credit rating agencies have also voiced confidence that Treasury would not risk a sovereign debt default, including Moody's and Fitch.[18]

Moreover, sovereign debt default should never be a primary concern during a temporary debt limit impasse. Congress has voted in support of several bills that would allow the Treasury to continue borrowing at the debt limit to meet debt service needs.[19] In the event that insufficient cash levels became a concern to meet federal debt obligations, Congress and the Administration could cooperate to remove at least this critical risk.

This has not happened likely because debt limit standoffs represent a game of chicken. Borrowing authority for debt limit service would defuse much of the tension inherent in current debt limit standoffs. Importantly, such authority would reduce executive leverage at the debt limit. The President's strongest hand in debt limit standoffs is to threaten default. Similar to the fable in which a child finally reveals to all that the emperor has no clothes, forcing the Administration to show its cards during a debt limit impasse may serve to focus on the real issue lawmakers should be debating: What reforms will we put in place to control spending and debt?

Another useful exercise would ask the congressional budget committees and the executive to present a prioritized annual cash budget. Assuming no borrowing, how would Congress and the executive prioritize among competing federal programs? This

---

[16]Government Accountability Office, "Letter to Senator Bob Packwood (R–OR)," October 9, 1985, http://www.gao.gov/products/449522#mt=e-report (accessed September 6, 2013).

[17]Peter Cook and Cheyenne Hopkins, "U.S. Contingency Plan Said to Give Priority to Bondholders," Bloomberg, July 28, 2011, http://www.bloomberg.com/news/2011-07-28/u-s-contingency-plan-gives-bondholders-priority.html (accessed September 6, 2013)

[18]Romina Boccia, "Moody's: Further Deficit Reduction Needed to Maintain Stable Outlook," The Foundry, July 23, 2013, http://blog.heritage.org/2013/07/23/moodys-further-deficit-reduction-needed-to-maintain-stable-outlook/, and Fitch Ratings, "Fitch Affirms United States at 'AAA'; Outlook Remains Negative," U.S. Medium-Term Fiscal Projections—An Update, June 28, 2013, http://www.fitchratings.com/creditdesk/reports/report_frame.cfm?rpt_id=711441 (accessed September 11, 2013; subscription required).

[19]Representative Tom McClintock (R–CA), "HR 807-Full Faith and Credit Act," February 25, 2013, https://www.congress.gov/bill/113th-congress/house-bill/807 (accessed January 28, 2016); Senator Pat Toomey (R–PA). "S.163 - Full Faith and Credit Act," January 26, 2011, https://www.congress.gov/bill/112th-congress/senate-bill/163 (accessed January 28, 2016); and Representative Tom McClintock (R–CA), "H.R. 692- Default Prevention Act," February 3, 2015, https://www.congress.gov/bill/114th-congress/house-bill/692 (accessed January 28, 2016).

would be a prudent exercise to reveal to the public what Congress and the executive considered to be the most important programs. It would also confront lawmakers and the public more directly with the important question of whether the things the federal government is borrowing for are truly necessary. Americans might ask twice whether a certain activity should take place when considering the impact on younger generations from borrowing for this or that purpose more specifically. In the event of a debt limit impasse, this cash budget could serve as guidance for prioritization of payments at the debt limit.

Desperate Times Call for Desperate Measures

The debt limit allows Congress to exercise its power of the purse in making vital course corrections when confronted with the results of unsustainable spending decisions. As such, the debt limit presents a decisive, action-forcing moment for Congress to take charge of the automatic spending increases that are driving the U.S. spending and debt crisis.

The fact that Congress has not been willing to force spending reforms does not lessen the importance of the debt limit as an action-forcing mechanism to prevent a future fiscal crisis. Congress should cut spending and reform the entitlement programs to put the budget on a path to balance before increasing the debt limit again.

Congress could avoid repeated debt limit panics by acting prudently and with enough foresight to address the federal government's spending and debt problems before the debt limit seemingly forces lawmakers to adopt bad policy. It is not the debt limit that is the problem. The problem is a lack of congressional and presidential leadership to address the root source of growing spending and debt: unsustainable spending growth in federal health care programs and Social Security.

Congress should modernize Medicare, Medicaid, and Social Security and empower people to exercise more choice in spending their health care and retirement dollars.

Congress's budget resolution included some important reforms in this direction. However, without additional legislation to implement the reforms in the congressional blueprint, spending will continue to grow out of control. Lawmakers should address the key drivers of spending growth and put the budget on a path to balance—before raising the debt limit. My colleagues and I at the Heritage Foundation laid out that path in detail in a recent report, which I submit for the congressional record.[20]

Thank you.

---

[20]Romina Boccia, Paul Winfree, Curtis Dubay, and Michael Sargent, "Blueprint for Congressional Fiscal Action in the Remainder of 2015," Heritage Foundation *Backgrounder* No. 3052, September 2, 2015, http://www.heritage.org/research/reports/2015/09/blueprint-for-congressional-fiscal-action-in-the-remainder-of-2015.

FUNDAMENTAL SPENDING REFORM: THE SOLUTION TO THE DEBT CEILING DEBATE

VERONIQUE DE RUGY

Senior Research Fellow, Mercatus Center at George Mason University

House Committee on Financial Services, Subcommittee on Oversight and Investigations
Hearing: Unsustainable Federal Spending and the Debt Limit

February 2, 2016

Chairman Duffy, Ranking Member Green, and members of the subcommittee: Thank you for the opportunity to testify today.

After offering a brief look at how we arrived at our current state, I would like to make the following points:

1. High and increasing debt has adverse consequences for our economy.

2. There are a number of institutional reforms that can be implemented to check the spending that drives this growth in debt.

3. Entitlement reform is essential, as rapidly burgeoning growth in entitlements is driving the growth in spending.

4. The latest increase in the debt ceiling gives us some time to reach an agreement that reflects real reform, and there are sufficient assets available that default is not a concern.

1. THE INCREASING FEDERAL DEBT

The origins of the federal government's statutory debt limit can be traced back to 1917, when the country borrowed money to finance World War I.[1] Limitations on federal borrowing were intended to control congressional spending by limiting the amount of debt that the federal government could accumulate. Policymakers have routinely

---

1. Congressional Research Service, "The Debt Limit: History and Recent Increases," October 1, 2015, 5.

For more information or to meet with the scholar, contact
Robin Walker, 202-550-9246, rwalker@mercatus.gmu.edu
Mercatus Center at George Mason University, 3434 Washington Blvd., 4th Floor, Arlington, Virginia 22201

pushed the debt limit ever higher ever since. Indeed, the limit has been increased almost 20 times since 1993,[2] and the federal debt has ballooned from less than $5 trillion to $19 trillion. That figure continues to rise, thanks to the Bipartisan Budget Act of 2015, which passed in October and suspended the debt limit until March 16, 2017.[3]

It is ironic that the suspension of the debt limit was part of a deal to increase spending above the Budget Control Act of 2011's intended spending caps (for the second time). Despite the popular perception of Republicans and Democrats caught in gridlock, the truth is that after the political dust settles, the end result is always the same: a bipartisan agreement on more spending and more debt.

This needs to change. According to the most recent 10-year fiscal forecast from the Congressional Budget Office (CBO), "federal outlays remain near 21 percent of GDP for the next few years—higher than their average of 20.2 percent over the past 50 years … [and] if current laws generally remained the same, growth in outlays would outstrip growth in the economy, and outlays would rise to 23 percent of GDP by 2026."[4]

CBO projections also show that federal debt held by the public will reach 76 percent of GDP by the end of 2016—a full two percentage points higher than 2014. It is also expected to grow from $14 trillion this year to $24 trillion by 2026.

That's probably an underestimate since it is a projection based on the assumption that policymakers will keep their promises to cut spending and raise taxes. Based on Congress's termination of the sequester years ahead of schedule and its historical propensity to spend more and more each year, such an assumption is unlikely to come true. The projections also assume that the economy will grow at current projected rates and without any recessions. This, too, is unlikely, since the country tends to go into recession every five to six years.

Deficits are also going to go up to $544 billion from last year's $439 billion. Over the coming decade, the size of the federal deficit will double to reach an annual gap of almost 5 percent of GDP. CBO predicts that deficits will total $9.4 trillion. That's up $1.5 trillion from its August report. It also notes that under the alternative scenario budget projection, spending will increase to 21.9 percent of GDP in 2020, to 25.8 percent in 2030, and to 30.4 percent in 2040.

The expansion of mandatory programs—such as Medicare, Medicaid, Affordable Care Act subsidies, and Social Security—is the driving force behind this spending growth and our exploding debt. These entitlements will trigger even higher levels of debt in the years outside the 10-year budget window.

Unfortunately, as the debt grows, the interest payments on that debt will grow as well. If the United States does not change course, interest on the debt will end up as one of its biggest budget items. Our unfunded liabilities keep going up, too. The net present value of the promises made to the American people for which the United States does not have the money to pay is roughly $75.5 trillion, according to the Treasury Department.

High debt levels are problematic. As CBO explained a few years ago,

> Such high and rising debt later in the coming decade would have serious negative consequences: When interest rates return to higher (more typical) levels, federal spending on interest payments would increase substantially. Moreover, because federal borrowing reduces national saving, over time the capital stock would be smaller and total wages would be lower than they would be if the debt was reduced. In addition, lawmakers would have less flexibility than they would have if debt levels were lower to use tax and spending policy to respond to unexpected challenges. Finally, a large debt increases the risk of a fiscal crisis, during which investors would lose so much confidence in the government's ability to manage its budget that the government would be unable to borrow at affordable rates.[5]

2. Ibid, 11.

3. Veronique de Rugy, "Budget Deal Is Business-as-Usual in Washington," Mercatus Center at George Mason University, November 18, 2015.

4. Congressional Budget Office, "The Budget and Economic Outlook: 2016 to 2026," January 2016, 4.

5. Congressional Budget Office, "Updated Budget Projections: Fiscal Years 2013 to 2023," May 2013.

These numbers are important to keep in mind when discussing the next debt ceiling deadline. Indeed, when March 2017 comes around we can expect that Washington will once again have the same debate it has had for the last few years about whether or not to raise the debt ceiling and under what circumstances. On one side you will find those who want to raise the limit without questions asked. On the other side, you will find those who will demand reforms in exchange for yet another increase in the debt ceiling.

Continuing to pass debt ceiling increases without proper spending reforms would be irresponsible. It is also irresponsible to signal to the international community that the US government could possibly default on its debt obligations while Washington works through whether it will raise the debt limit before or after it formulates a plan to reduce government spending.

WHAT'S AT STAKE

To be sure, default should not be an option on the table. However, raising the debt ceiling without a commitment to improve our long-term debt problem has adverse consequences. In 2011, the rating agency Fitch warned the US government that while it supported raising the debt ceiling, it also wanted the government to come up with a credible medium-term deficit-reduction plan.[6] Other rating agencies at the time also warned the United States of the negative consequences of not dealing with the country's long-term debt.

If Congress does not address our debt problem before March 2017, the optimal outcome would then be to raise the debt limit while Congress and the president pass a credible plan to reduce near- and long-term spending at the same time.

Fortunately, if an agreement to control spending and raise the debt limit is not reached, the United States need not risk defaulting on its debt. The Treasury Department has the legal authority to prioritize interest payments on the debt above all other obligations, whether that means delaying payments to contractors or managing other obligations. But Congress should not be forced to raise the debt ceiling under false pretenses.

As was the case in 2011, the United States will have enough expected cash flow (tax revenue) and assets on hand to avoid either of these unattractive options. Managing payments in this manner is by no means optimal, and Treasury officials have indicated that this will be difficult owing to payment automation. That said, it is important to recognize the options that are available to prevent a default. While Washington has difficult choices to make, defaulting on its debt obligations should not be part of the discussion about how to handle the debt limit or reduce long-term government spending.

2. REAL INSTITUTIONAL REFORM

The heated rhetoric coming in March 2017 about whether Congress should raise the debt ceiling will obscure the federal government's real problem: an unprecedented increase in government spending and the future explosion of entitlement spending has created a fiscal imbalance today and for the years to come. No matter what Congress decides to do about the debt ceiling, the United States must implement institutional reforms that constrain government spending and return the country to a sustainable fiscal position.

Real institutional reforms, as opposed to onetime cuts, would change the trajectory of fiscal policy and put the United States on a more sustainable path. Such reforms could include:

1. *A constitutional amendment to limit spending.* The inability of lawmakers to constrain their own spending makes spending limits enforced through the US Constitution preferable.[7]

6. Veronique de Rugy, "Policy Implications of the S&P Warnings," *The Corner, National Review*, July 22, 2011. Also see Jeannette Neumann, "Fitch Unveils Two Possible Routes to Downgrading US Debt Rating," *Wall Street Journal*, January 15, 2013.
7. David M. Primo, "Constitution Is Only Way to Cut US Deficit," *Bloomberg Business*, February 24, 2011.

2. *Meaningful budget reforms that limit lawmakers' tendency to spend.* In the absence of constitutional rules, budget rules should have broad scope, few and high-hurdle escape clauses, and minimal accounting discretion.[8]

3. *The end of budget gimmicks.* Creative bookkeeping is at the center of many countries' financial troubles. Congress should institute a transparent budget process and end abuse of the emergency spending rule, reliance on overly rosy scenarios, and all other gimmicks.[9]

4. *A strict cut-as-you-go system.* This system should apply to the entire federal budget, not just to a small portion of it. There should be no new spending without offsetting cuts.[10]

5. *A BRAC-like commission for discretionary spending.* Commissions composed of independent experts often tackle intractable political problems successfully.[11]

3. REAL ENTITLEMENT REFORMS

As mentioned earlier, the drivers of our future debt are spending on Medicare, Medicaid, Affordable Care Act subsidies, and Social Security. Without reforms today, vast tax increases will be needed to pay for the unfunded promises made to a steadily growing cohort of seniors.

While economists disagree when it comes to fiscal policy, a consensus has emerged that spending-based fiscal adjustments are not only more likely to reduce the debt-to-GDP ratio than tax-based ones but are also less likely to trigger a recession.[12] In fact, if accompanied by the right type of policies (especially changes to public employees' pay and public pension reforms), spending-based adjustments can actually be associated with economic growth.

Fortunately, numerous workable solutions are available to lawmakers, including adding a system of personal savings accounts to Social Security, liberalizing medical savings accounts, and making the latter permanent to reduce healthcare costs by increasing competition between providers and making consumers more responsive to tradeoffs.[13]

These options are supposed to encourage families to save more and also to use their money more responsibly and in a manner more consistent with their long-term needs. And since taxpayers remain in control of their cash, they can also pass it along if they don't use it all before they die—giving the next generation a head start when it comes to building assets.

Better yet, we should free the healthcare supply from the many constraints imposed by federal and state governments and the special interests they serve.[14] The stakes are high: Bringing revolutionary innovation to this industry could mean not just bending the healthcare cost curve but breaking it to bits—making the need for health insurance much less important, if not moot, in many cases.

8. David M. Primo, "Making Budget Rules Bite" (Mercatus on Policy, Mercatus Center at George Mason University, Arlington, VA, March 2010).

9. Veronique de Rugy, "Budget Gimmicks or the Destructive Art of Creative Accounting" (Mercatus Working Paper, Mercatus Center at George Mason University, Arlington, VA, June 2010).

10. Veronique de Rugy and David Bieler, "Is PAYGO a No-Go?" (Mercatus on Policy, Mercatus Center at George Mason University, Arlington, VA, April 2010).

11. Jerry Brito, "The BRAC Model for Spending Reform" (Mercatus on Policy, Mercatus Center at George Mason University, Arlington, VA, February 2010).

12. Veronique de Rugy, "The Effect of Tax Increases and Spending Cuts on Economic Growth" (Testimony before the Senate Committee on the Budget, Mercatus Center at George Mason University, Arlington, VA, May 22, 2013).

13. Chris Edwards and Tad DeHaven, "War Between Generations: Federal Spending on the Elderly Set to Explode" (Policy Analysis No. 488, Cato Institute, Washington, DC, September 16, 2003).

14. Robert Graboyes, "Fortress and Frontier in American Health Care" (Mercatus Research, Mercatus Center at George Mason University, Arlington, VA, October 2014).

4. REVENUE AND ASSETS AVAILABLE TO FUND OUR COMMITMENT UNTIL AN AGREEMENT IS REACHED

With that in mind, let's think about what happens in March 2017. At that time, the government will reach the debt ceiling, and the Treasury will no longer be able to issue federal debt. The federal government could reduce spending, increase federal revenues by a corresponding amount to cover the gap, or find other funding mechanisms. This would allow time for Congress and the president to reach an agreement to change the country's financial path before raising the debt ceiling.

At that time, the Treasury Department will have several financial management options to continue paying the government's obligations. These include (1) prioritizing payments;[15] (2) taking financial steps, including permitting the suspension of investments in, and the redemption of securities held by, certain government trust funds or postponing the sale of nonmarketable debt;[16] (3) liquidating some assets to pay government bills;[17] and (4) using the Social Security Trust Fund to continue paying Social Security benefits.[18]

PRIORITIZING PAYMENTS

The Secretary of the Treasury has long-standing authority to prioritize payments and does not have to pay bills in the order in which they are received. The US Government Accountability Office found that

> the Secretary of the Treasury has the authority to determine the order in which obligations are to be paid should the Congress fail to raise the statutory debt ceiling and revenues are inadequate to cover all required payments. There is no statute or other basis for concluding that the Treasury must pay outstanding obligations in the order they are presented for payment. Treasury is free to liquidate obligations in any order it determines will best serve the interests of the United States.[19]

According to a report by the Treasury Department's Inspector General (IG), during the 2011 debt ceiling crisis the Treasury "considered a range of options with respect to how Treasury would operate if the debt ceiling was not raised." Further, the report notes that Treasury officials told the IG that "organizationally they viewed the option of delaying payments as the least harmful among the options under review" and that "the decision of how Treasury would have operated if the U.S. had exhausted its borrowing authority would have been made by the President in consultation with the Secretary of the Treasury."[20]

TEMPORARY MEASURES

During the last debt ceiling debate in 2011, my colleague Jason Fichtner and I listed all the assets that Treasury could tap into to avoid a default until an agreement between the president and Congress be reached.[21] We updated this report in 2013.[22] At the time we explained that Treasury was expected to collect $2.6 trillion in revenue. We wrote:

> That alone would be enough to cover interest on the debt ($218 billion), thereby avoiding any technical default of the US government on its debt obligations to Social Security ($809 billion), Medicare

15. Jason J. Fichtner and Veronique de Rugy, "The Debt Ceiling: What Is at Stake?" (Mercatus Research, Mercatus Center at George Mason University, Arlington, VA, April 2011).

16. Veronique de Rugy and Jason J. Fichtner, "The Debt Limit Debate" (Mercatus on Policy, Mercatus Center at George Mason University, Arlington, VA, May 2011).

17. Fichtner and de Rugy, "The Debt Ceiling: What Is at Stake?"

18. The Social Security Trust Funds can only be used to pay Social Security benefits. See Glenn Kessler, "Can President Obama Keep Paying Social Security Benefits Even If the Debt Ceiling Is Reached?," *Washington Post*, July 13, 2011; Contract with America Advancement Act of 1996, Pub. L. No. 104-121 (1996).

19. US Government Accountability Office, Letter to Senator Bob Packwood, October 9, 1985.

20. Department of the Treasury, Office of Inspector General, Letter to Senator Orrin G. Hatch, OIG-CA-12-006, August 24, 2012.

21. Fichtner and de Rugy, "The Debt Ceiling: What Is at Stake?"

22. Jason J. Fichtner and Veronique de Rugy, "The Debt Ceiling: Assets Available to Prevent Default" (Mercatus Research, Mercatus Center at George Mason University, Arlington, VA, January 2013).

($581 billion), and Medicaid ($267 billion), and it would leave approximately $725 billion for other priorities.

In addition, we noted that the Treasury Department had financial measures at its disposal to fund government operations temporarily without having to issue new debt. To be clear, our list was only meant to present the range of possible options available to Congress. But, as we noted then, those may not be good or desirable options.

These assets totaled $1.9 trillion and included $50.2 billion in nonrestricted cash on hand,[23] $121.1 billion in restricted cash and other monetary assets (gold, international monetary assets, foreign currency),[24] and the redemption of existing investments in other trust funds.[25]

We also noted that the government could rely on the determination of a "debt issuance suspension period." This determination would permit the redemption of existing, and the suspension of new, investments of the Civil Service Retirement and Disability Fund (CSRDF).[26] Right now there is $858.7 billion intergovernmental holdings in the CSRDF.

In March 2017, the numbers will be different, but the same assets may be used to avoid a default. Relying on any of these sources of funds or increasing the debt ceiling without reducing existing budget commitments illustrates the irresponsible path the country is on and the urgent need for institutional spending reform. Nonetheless, these assets could be used as a temporary measure to allow Congress and the administration to negotiate spending reductions and institutional reforms to the budget process to ensure the nation is put back on a sound fiscal path.

Thank you. I am happy to take your questions.

23. Department of the Treasury, "Daily Treasury Statement," January 14, 2013.
24. Department of the Treasury, *2012 Financial Report of the US Government*, 65. At the time, the Treasury owned approximately 261.4 million ounces of gold and marked the value of its gold holdings at $42 per ounce, giving a reported value of $11.1 billion. At a spot market price of $1,500 per ounce, Treasury's gold holdings could be valued near $400 billion.
25. Department of the Treasury, "Monthly Statement of the Public Debt of the United States," December 31, 2015.
26. In September 1985, the Treasury took the step of disinvesting the Civil Service Retirement and Disability Trust Fund, the Social Security Trust Funds, and several smaller trust funds.

Unsustainable Federal Spending and the Debt Limit

Our government's good credit is vital to everything it does.

There are two ways to wreck that credit: by borrowing too much or by failing to pay it back on time and in full.

Congress alone has the constitutional power to tax, to borrow and to spend. We regulate our borrowing through the debt limit. When we need to increase it, we have a duty to review and revise the policies that are driving that debt.

The United States now staggers under $19 trillion of debt, nearly half of it run up in the last eight years. The interest on that debt is the fastest growing component of the federal budget – within five years it will consume more than what we now spend for defense. That's why we dare not increase the debt without also addressing what is driving it. But that can often lead to a temporary impasse.

When that happens, it is vital that credit markets maintain supreme confidence in the security of their loans. Otherwise, the interest rates that lenders charge us would quickly rise to account for the increased risk and our precarious budget situation could rapidly spin out of control.

The organic law that established the Treasury Department in 1789 specifically says, "It shall be the duty of the Secretary of the Treasury to digest and prepare plans for the improvement and management of the revenue, and for the support of public credit." " MANAGE the revenue and support the public credit." The GAO clearly spelled out what that means in answering the Senate Finance Committee in 1985: "Treasury is free to liquidate obligations in any order it finds will best serve the interests of the United States." The Constitution commands that "the public debt is not to be questioned," and this is the practical mechanism for it. Most state constitutions provide that first call on any revenues is to maintain and protect their sovereign credit.

That brings us to the fine point of the problem. In recent years, the Treasury Department has denied that it has either the ability or the authority to do so.

We now know from documents recently uncovered by this committee that this was a deliberate and calculated lie told to increase political pressure on Congress. These documents reveal that Federal Reserve officials were incredulous and appalled that the administration would make such statements, because they ran a severe risk of panicking credit markets.

We also now know the Treasury department actually was preparing contingency plans to prioritize debt at the same time the Treasury secretary was denying it was possible.

In 2011, I first introduced legislation to place an affirmative duty on the Treasury Department to provide first claim on any revenues for debt service. Ironically, the same Treasury Secretary who claimed he lacked legal authority opposed this bill that explicitly gave him that legal authority. In response to his untruthful claim it was not possible, we amended the bill in 2013 simply to allow the Treasury Secretary to borrow above the debt limit to guarantee that the debt would be paid in full and on time. It passed the House in 2013 and again last year.

Opponents argued that this put creditors like China ahead of paying troops in the field. Actually, most of our debt is to Americans, and without our credit we can't pay our troops or anybody else. By protecting our credit *first*, we actually support and maintain our ability to pay for *all* of our other obligations.

The President said this is tantamount to a family saying it would make its house payment but not its car payment. Both are bad. But let's continue the analogy. If the family is living on its credit cards as we are, it had better make the minimum payment on its credit card first, or it won't be able to pay the rest of its bills.

And when that family has to increase its credit limit because it's spending above its means, it had better have a serious conversation about what's driving its debt and what to do about it.

Principled disputes over HOW the debt limit is addressed are going to happen from time to time. Just a few years ago, then-Senator Barack Obama vigorously opposed an increase in the debt limit sought by the Bush administration.

When these controversies erupt – as they inevitably do in a free society – it is imperative that credit markets are supremely confident that their loans to the United States are secure.

Unsustainable Federal Spending and the Debt Limit

Testimony to Subcommittee on Oversight and Investigations

House Financial Service Committee

Daniel J. Mitchell

Senior Fellow, Cato Institute

February 2, 2016

Mr. Chairman and members of the Subcommittee, my name is Daniel Mitchell and I'm a Senior Fellow at the Cato Institute. Thank you for the opportunity to present my views on the very important issue of America's fiscal outlook and the role of the debt limit.

1. The United States has a serious long-run spending problem

Most people understand that our nation faces very serious long-run fiscal challenges thanks to changing demographics and poorly designed entitlement programs. We routinely get grim estimates from the Congressional Budget Office, the Office of Management and Budget, the Government Accountability Office, as well as private forecasters.

Most of these estimates focus on red ink, specifically what's happening to annual deficits in addition to what's happening to aggregate levels of publicly-held debt. This is useful information, but it's important to understand that red ink generally should be viewed as a symptom. The real issue is the overall burden of government spending because that's what requires the diversion of resources from the productive sector of the economy, regardless of whether outlays are financed by taxes, borrowing, or printing money.

It's also best to focus on government spending because projections of ever-larger levels of long-run debt are entirely the result of ever-expanding amounts of federal spending, not inadequate tax receipts.

Here are some numbers from a recent CBO forecast, which show that tax revenues already are above their long-run average and that the tax burden – even without any legislated tax hikes – will gradually increase over the next few decades. This is due to the fact that some parts of the tax code are not indexed for inflation and also because even modest levels of economic growth gradually push people into higher tax brackets.

Projected Revenues, Compared With Past Averages

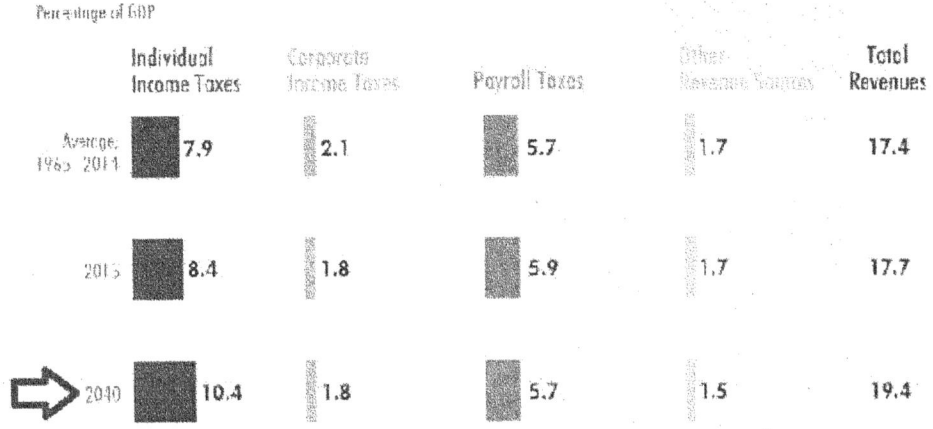

Percentage of GDP

	Individual Income Taxes	Corporate Income Taxes	Payroll Taxes	Other Revenue Sources	Total Revenues
Average, 1965-2014	7.9	2.1	5.7	1.7	17.4
2015	8.4	1.8	5.9	1.7	17.7
2040	10.4	1.8	5.7	1.5	19.4

Under current law revenues would equal 19.4 percent of GDP by 2040, CBO projects, compared with an average of 17.4 percent of GDP over the past 50 years. A boost in receipts from individual income taxes accounts for the rise in total revenues; receipts from all other sources, taken together, are projected to decline slightly as a percentage of GDP.

The numbers tell a very clear story. Taxes will slowly but surely claim a larger share of our output over time, but government debt levels are projected to increase because the burden of government spending will grow even faster, consuming an ever-larger portion of the economy's output. As noted above, this is primarily the result of entitlement programs that resemble Ponzi schemes, combined with demographic change, specifically an aging population and falling birthrate that will cause a population pyramid to become a population cylinder.

In some sense, we're on a path to becoming a failed European-style welfare state. But the numbers may tell an even more depressing story. Various international bureaucracies put together apples-to-apples projections of long-run fiscal status.

This chart is from a study by the International Monetary Fund looking at fiscal challenges in varying nations. The vertical axis captures the degree to which age-related outlays will increase by 2030 and the horizontal axis is an estimate of the amount of fiscal consolidation (as a share of GDP) that will be necessary to stabilize government debt burdens. It's not good to be in the upper-right quadrant and the United States arguably is in a worse position than any other nation.

62

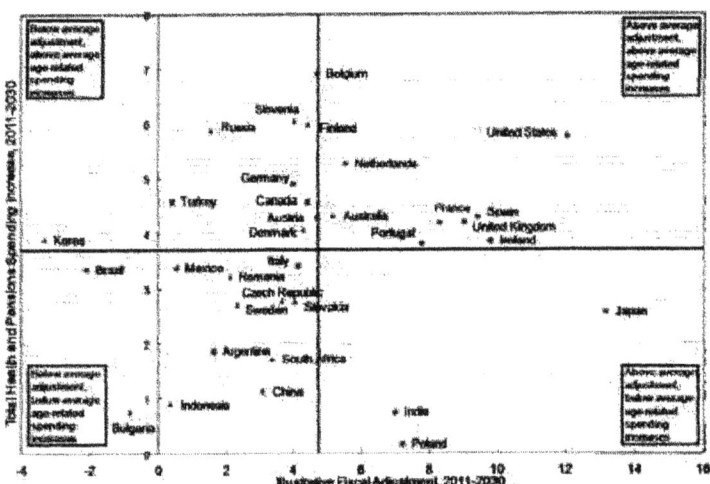

Figure 14. Illustrative Fiscal Adjustment and Projected Age-Related Spending Increases in 2011–2030 (in percent of GDP)

Source: IMF staff estimates and projections; IMF (2010c).

Note: Fiscal adjustment refers to improvement in the cyclically adjusted primary balance needed to achieve the illustrative gross government debt target. Circles indicate debt ratios above 60 percent for advanced economies and 40 percent for emerging economies, projected at end-2012 (higher debt); triangles indicate debt ratios below 60 percent for advanced economies and 40 percent for emerging economies, projected for the same period (lower debt). See note in Figure 11 for further details. The vertical and horizontal lines represent unweighted averages.

For Australia, the figures do not take into account the federal government budget, released on May 11, which envisages a return to federal government surpluses by 2012/13. For Greece (not shown), the illustrative 2011–30 adjustment need is 9.2 percent of GDP, after measures of 7.6 percent of GDP undertaken in 2010. This increase in health and pension spending is projected at 7.6 percent of GDP.

Here are the latest estimates from the Organization for Economic Cooperation and Development, which show the amount of annual fiscal consolidation that would be necessary to stabilize debt levels by 2030. In the developed world, only three nations have a bigger long-run problem than the United States.

Figure 1.12. Budgetary consolidation requirements to reduce government debt to 60% of GDP
Average change in the underlying primary balance (2010-2030), percentage points of GDP

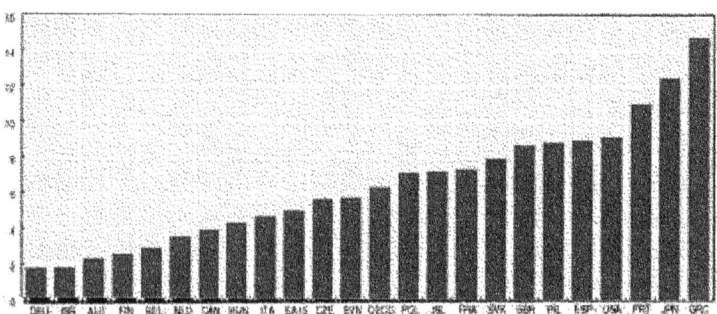

Note: The average measure of consolidation is the difference between the underlying primary balance in 2010 and the average underlying primary balance between 2015 and 2030, except for those countries for which the debt target is only achieved after 2030, in which case the average is calculated up until the year that the debt target is achieved.
Source: OECD (2013), OECD Economic Outlook 93 Long-Term Database.

StatLink http://dx.doi.org/10.1787/888932983870

Last but not least, here is an estimate of future government debt from the Bank for International Settlements. The red line is the baseline forecast and the blue and green lines show debt levels based on assumptions of varying degrees of fiscal reform. Of the major economies reviewed in the study, only Japan had worse numbers than the United States.

United States

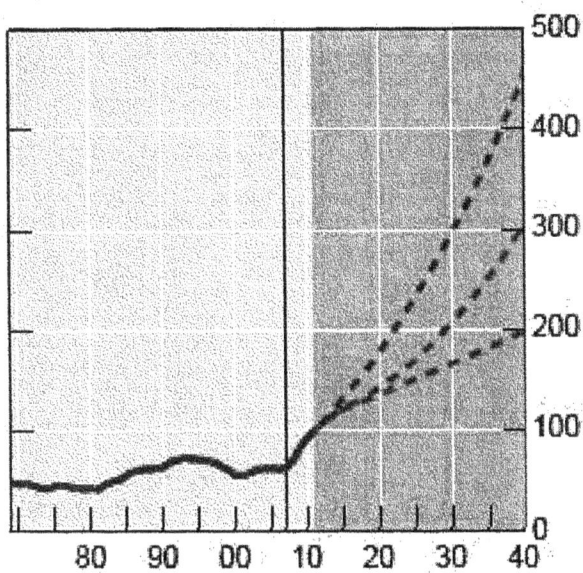

For what it's worth, I think these forecasts from the IMF, OECD, and BIS are actually too pessimistic, at least in that I would not want to trade places with countries like France or Italy. The long-run numbers for the United States are bad because of the assumption that spending will climb dramatically and revenues will stay constant, and this leads to compounding levels of government debt. But that problem is actually simple to solve with some sort of spending cap.

But for many of Europe's welfare states, the burden of government spending already exceeds 50 percent of economic output and tax burdens have been pushed close to – or even beyond – revenue-maximizing levels. That problem is much harder to solve.

2. The debt limit is an appropriate vehicle for legislation

While there is presumably near-universal recognition that the United States has major long-run challenges, there is not agreement on how to solve the problem. And there may be even less consensus on whether the debt limit should be used as an action-forcing vehicle for fiscal reform.

In part, this is partisan posturing and conventional executive-vs-legislature game playing. All Administrations, regardless of party, dislike fights over debt limits and prefer "clean" legislation. And both parties in Congress, when the White House is controlled by the other side, like to attach conditions and create obstacles.

Setting aside these political aspects, there is a strong case for using must-pass pieces of legislation as a means to an end. Simply stated, it beats the alternative of doing nothing.

Consider this example. Greece is now suffering through a very deep recession, with record unemployment and harsh economic conditions. Wouldn't it have been preferable if there was some sort of mechanism, say, 15 or 25 years ago that would have enabled some lawmakers to throw sand in the gears so that the government couldn't issue any more debt? Yes, there would have been some budgetary turmoil at the time, but it would have been trivial compared to the misery the Greek people currently are enduring.

Let's now apply this reasoning to the United States. We know we're on an unsustainable path. Do we want to wait until we hit a crisis before we address the over-spending crisis? Or do we want to take prudent and modest steps today – such as reasonable entitlement reform and spending caps – to ensure prosperity and long-run growth?

The second option is much better. Yet since those steps won't be popular with interest groups, it's quite possible that they can only be imposed in the unusual circumstances that surround debt-limit legislation.

With this in mind, it would be useful to offer a response to the July 2015 GAO report on the debt limit and proposed alternatives. GAO basically concluded that that it would be best to have automatic or near-automatic increases in the debt limit, mostly because of a finding that uncertainty in financial markets can cause small increases in interest rates for government debt. And since there's a lot of government debt, even a small increase can add tens of millions of dollars to the fiscal burden.

All that may be true, but GAO was looking at a tree and ignoring the forest. The issue is not whether fights over the debt limit may cause hiccups in the short run. What matters is whether fights over debt limits may produce reforms that avert catastrophic consequences in the long run.

3. A debt limit fight would only lead to default if an Administration wanted default

The more common argument against using the debt limit to force reform is that it is akin to playing with fire and may lead to default. And that would be potentially catastrophic to financial markets rather than a mere hiccup.

Predictions of doom almost certainly are overheated, but it doesn't matter because there is more than enough tax revenue to ensure that the federal government can honor its contractual obligation to bondholders. If we assume the next debt limit is reached in 2017, it's very difficult to see how a default may occur since projected revenues that year will be more than $3.5 trillion, more than 11 times greater than the projected interest payments for 2017, which CBO says will total $308 billion.

Some argue that prioritizing interest payments would be impossible or impractical for a couple of reasons. First, they say Treasury doesn't have the legal power to prioritize payments, so if the debt limit wasn't increased (which would be akin to an immediate balanced-budget requirement), the department would face chaos and a default would be an inevitable consequence. But this is nonsense because the law does not micromanage Treasury operations, and it certainly does not prohibit "prioritization."

The second – and more common – argument is that Treasury has the power to prioritize in a spend-only-what-you-collect world, but that it lacks the competence. This is a specious argument since many state and local governments routinely delay payments to vendors and other beneficiaries when money is tight. Suffice to say that if notoriously mismanaged states such as California and Illinois can figure it out, then there's no reason not to expect a similar level of performance from Treasury officials.

Indeed, one must assume that Treasury already has contingency plans for such a possibility, and this Committee's work seems to have confirmed this suspicion.

Finally, I will close by noting that utterly disingenuous Administration tactic of trying to blur the difference between contractual obligations to bondholders and promises to give money to various interest groups. Treasury officials and others use deceptive and misleading language about defaulting on commitments/promises/etc to make it seem as if delaying payments of things like crop subsidies and Medicaid reimbursements is somehow equivalent to default on interest payments.

Thank you for your attention and I look forward to any questions.

Rep. Mark Pocan (WI-02) Opening Statement

O&I Subcommittee Hearing: "Unsustainable Federal Spending and the Debt Limit"

I want to thank Members of the Subcommittee, including Chairman Duffy and Ranking Member Green, for allowing me to testify today. I also want to thank Ranking Member Waters, for inviting me to participate in today's hearing. As a Member of the Budget Committee I have a particular interest in the discussion of our fiscal policy and look forward to answering your questions here today.

In Congress, there is a tendency to ignore long term consequences in favor of temporary, short term victories. This mentality is no more evident than in the approach of my Republican colleagues when it comes to fiscal policy, specifically their heavy-handed approach to cutting government spending and deficit reduction.

As a small business owner for over 25 years, I understand how difficult it is to run a business when the constant threat of a government shutdown or default creates panic and uncertainty among banks, investors and customers. Putting small business and consumer confidence at risk, at a time when both on the rise, to play political football here in Washington is just wrong. Worse, a default would see American families' hard-earned retirement savings lost, seniors and veterans could face delays in the monthly Social Security and disability checks they rely on, and the costs of homes and student loan rates could dramatically increase due to higher interest rates.

Even entertaining the idea of using the debt limit as a tool for forcing future across the board cuts is labeled as absurd by the majority of economists and a default would have devastating consequences for our economy and workforce. Refusing to raise the debt limit would constitute nothing short of fiscal malpractice, potentially reducing GDP by 20 to 30 percent and doubling the unemployment rate. We need to stop flirting with threatening the full faith and credit of the United States every time it is politically expedite. Over the past twelve months, private employment has risen by 2.6 million and employment is at 5 percent, its lowest rate since April 2008. For fiscally-minded Republicans who want to continue to promote economic growth and create good-paying jobs for hard working Americans, this should be a huge deterrent to even approaching another fiscal cliff.

This past December marked the 5th anniversary of the bipartisan Simpson-Bowles plan to reduce the deficit. This plan proposed massive cuts which were largely realized during the subsequent Budget Control Act's mindless approach to cutting known as sequestration.

I think something that gets lost in this debate on reducing the deficit is that lawmakers have enacted more than 70 percent of nondefense discretionary cuts proposed by the Simpson-Bowles Deficit Reduction plan which gave way to the years of steep budget cuts we've endured.

For the past few years, we have accepted massive budget cuts to research at universities, the National Institute for Health, Head Start, and to programs that provide a vital social safety net to our most vulnerable citizens. However, in the past five years, lawmakers have generated less than a third of the revenue recommended by the commission. A key tenet of the Simpson-Bowles plan was to strike a balance between cutting spending and raising revenue. Unfortunately, House Republicans have insisted on a heavy-handed approach to curtailing discretionary spending without generating enough revenue. This laser-like focus on short term cuts in discretionary spending, a relatively small portion of the federal budget, has put us on an unsustainable path for long term deficit reduction.

I believe it is vital to have an open and frank discussion on our nation's fiscal policy, but it must be done in a fashion which does not muddle the true nature of our spending priorities and mask self-imposed fiscal crisis in the guise of a tool to dictate fiscal discipline. We've cut all we can – to insinuate that federal budgets have been anything but austere in recent years is entirely misleading.

What is needed instead is the commonsense, balanced approach to deficit reduction that includes many options for generating revenue, such as some of the suggestions in the Simpson-Bowles plan. My Republican colleagues have been happy to make all the cuts, but have failed to seek out any revenue. But, as families sitting around the kitchen table trying to pay their mortgage or send their kids to college understand, there are two sides to balancing a budget: what we take in and what we spend and we are no different.

Again, thank you for having me participate in today's hearing and I look forward to taking your questions.

Center on Budget and Policy Priorities

820 First Street NE, Suite 510
Washington, DC 20002

Tel: 202-408-1080
Fax: 202-408-1056

center@cbpp.org
www.cbpp.org

February 2, 2016

Federal Spending and the Debt Limit
Testimony of Chad Stone, Chief Economist,
Center on Budget and Policy Priorities,
Before the Subcommittee on Oversight and Investigations
of the Financial Services Committee
U.S. House of Representatives

Chairman Duffy, Ranking Member Green, and other members of the subcommittee, thank you for the opportunity to testify at today's hearing. In my testimony I want to make two broad points. The first is the need to focus not just on spending but also on revenues in addressing our long-term budget challenges. The second is to caution strongly against thinking that the statutory limit on federal debt has any constructive role to play in addressing those challenges.

Budget deficits result from an imbalance between spending *and* revenue; rising debt relative to the size of the economy results from persistent large deficits, not from too much spending per se. Any plausible amount of spending to meet society's needs is sustainable if there are sufficient revenues to avoid large deficits.

CBO projects that under current tax and spending policies, rising debt will *ultimately* prove unsustainable. This poses a serious challenge to policymakers. At the same time, as I discuss in the first part of this testimony, there is not an immediate crisis. Policymakers, however, will have to make hard choices in setting a future course that is both fiscally responsible and realistic about the levels of spending and taxes appropriate to the country's needs.

These decisions need to be kept separate from the debt limit. As I discuss in the second part of the testimony, the debt limit encourages reckless brinkmanship that makes it harder to work out the compromises necessary to achieve a sustainable deficit-reduction agreement. As former Federal Reserve Chairman Ben Bernanke says in his recent book: "Refusing to raise the debt limit takes the economic well-being of the country hostage [and] ought to be unacceptable no matter what the underlying issue being contested."

I'll elaborate on these themes in the remainder of my testimony.

Trends in Government Spending and Debt

1. Temporary Factors Drove Deficits and Debt in the Great Recession

The sharp increases in deficits and debt during the financial crisis and Great Recession certainly caught policymakers' and the public's attention, but looking over a longer time span shows they were not unprecedented. Deficits were larger and the run-up in debt much sharper in World War II.

Budget Deficits and Debt Held by the Public

Percent of GDP

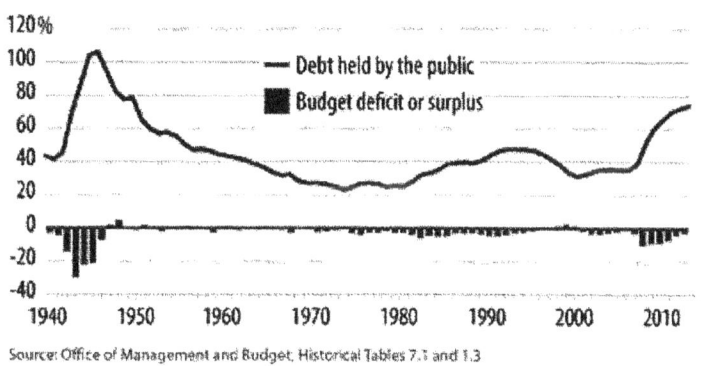

Source: Office of Management and Budget, Historical Tables 7.1 and 1.3

CENTER ON BUDGET AND POLICY PRIORITIES | CBPP.ORG

The surge in deficits after 2008, in fact, was temporary and resulted from economic weakness in the Great Recession as revenues shrank with the decline in economic activity, spending on unemployment insurance and other programs rose, and emergency tax cuts and spending increases were enacted to combat the recession. After peaking in 2009, the budget deficit fell as a share of GDP each year through 2015 as the economy slowly recovered, stimulus programs phased out, and policymakers enacted new deficit-reduction policies.

That decline is now over, and CBO's latest projections see deficits beginning to widen again and debt reaching 86 percent of GDP in 2026 — which, it is worth noting, is still well short of 1946's 106 percent.

2. The Aging of the Population and Rising Health Care Costs Are the Drivers of Longer-term Spending Increases

Even before the Great Recession, budget experts recognized that long-term deficits and debt were on an unsustainable path after about 2020 due to the aging of the population and expected increases in health care costs.[1] These factors are the drivers of projected future deficits and debt, not the

---

[1] Richard Kogan, *et al.*, "The Long-Term Fiscal Outlook is Bleak," Center on Budget and Policy Priorities, January 29, 2007, http://www.cbpp.org//sites/default/files/atoms/files/1-29-07bud.pdf.

temporary policies enacted to combat the recession,[2] which, in fact, kept economic conditions from being even worse than they were.[3]

In other words, in the lead-up to the debt-limit crisis and enactment of the Budget Control Act of 2011, policymakers faced a known long-term fiscal sustainability problem but not an immediate deficit or debt crisis. Notwithstanding policymakers' failure at that time to come up with a comprehensive long-term budget plan, things are substantially better now than they were then due to a combination of policy actions and projected slower growth in health care costs.

In 2010, budget experts were projecting that under plausible baseline assumptions, debt would rise well above 200 percent of GDP by 2040. CBO now projects that with no further action it could rise to 155 percent of GDP in 2046, citing the aging of the population and growth in per capita health care spending as main drivers. As CBO says, such a trend is ultimately unsustainable.

We should be clear, however, that we don't have a general problem of spending growing faster than the economy throughout the government. Program (non-interest) spending outside of Social Security and Medicare is running below its historical average, as a percent of GDP and is expected to fall further. The nearby charts show a distinct but temporary bump in such spending during the Great Recession and ensuing recovery, but that spending has already come down to below its historical average and is projected to decline further.

It is also important to remember that Social Security and Medicare are not bloated, unpopular programs. Large majorities of Americans say that they don't mind paying for Social Security because they value it for themselves, their families, and millions of others who rely on it. While Social Security benefits are more modest than many people realize, for most workers Social Security will be their only source of guaranteed retirement income that is not subject to investment risk or financial market fluctuations.[4]

Medicare is similarly popular and effective. In a nationally representative survey, more than three-quarters of respondents (77 percent) say Medicare is a very important program, ranking just below Social Security (83 percent).[5] Medicare's benefits, too, are not overly generous: they are less comprehensive than a typical employer-sponsored health plan, and Medicare households spend a substantially larger share of their budgets on out-of-pocket health costs and do non-Medicare households.

---

[2] Kathy Ruffing and Joel Friedman, "Economic Downturn and Legacy of Bush Policies Continue to Drive Large Budget Deficits," Center on Budget and Policy Priorities, February 28, 2013, http://www.cbpp.org/research/economic-downturn-and-legacy-of-bush-policies-continue-to-drive-large-deficits.

[3] Alan S. Blinder and Mark Zandi, "The Financial Crisis: Lessons for the Next One," Center on Budget and Policy Priorities, October 15, 2015, http://www.cbpp.org/research/economy/the-financial-crisis-lessons-for-the-next-one.

[4] "Policy Basics: Top Ten Facts About Social Security," Center on Budget and Policy Priorities, updated August 13, 2015, http://www.cbpp.org/research/social-security/policy-basics-top-ten-facts-about-social-security#_ftn28.

[5] "Medicare and Medicaid at 50," The Henry J. Kaiser Family Foundation, July 17, 2015, http://kff.org/medicaid/poll-finding/medicare-and-medicaid-at-50/.

Increasing generosity of benefits is not what's driving the increase in Social Security and Medicare spending. Rather it's the rising share of the population eligible for benefits, and in Medicare, rising health care costs — which affect public and private health care spending alike. Relatively modest changes would place Social Security on a sound financial footing for 75 years and beyond. The cost controls and delivery system reforms in the Affordable Care Act (ACA), plus other developments in health care delivery, are expected to curb (though not eliminate) health care cost pressure.

Non-Interest Spending Outside of Social Security and Medicare Below Historical Average

Spending as a percent of GDP

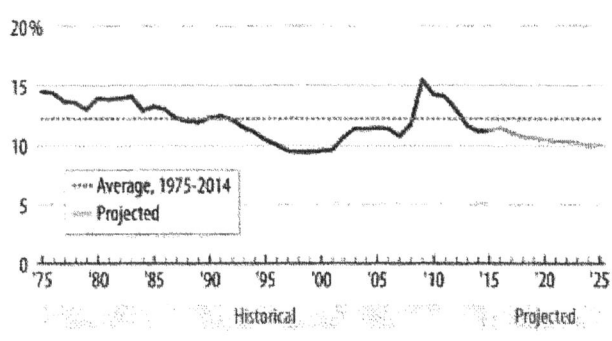

Source: OMB through 2014; CBPP analysis of CBO data thereafter

cbpp.org

Non-Interest Spending Outside Medicare and Social Security Set to Fall in Coming Decade

Spending as a percent of GDP

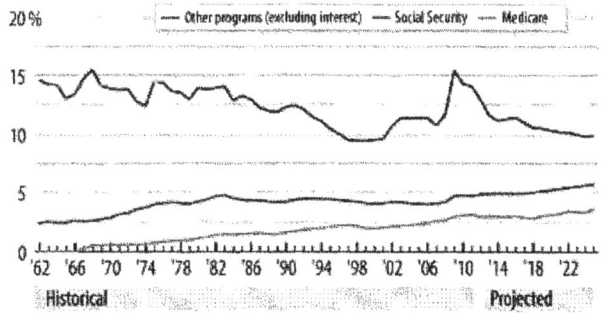

Source: OMB through 2014; CBPP analysis of CBO data thereafter

cbpp.org

3. Spending for Low-Income Programs Is Not Driving Deficits and Debt

A similar theme applies with regard to low-income programs. Spending on the most vulnerable among us rose sharply in the Great Recession and the years immediately thereafter, but CBPP analysis finds that spending on such programs outside health care has been falling and is projected to fall further. Specifically, outside of health care, federal spending for low-income programs (including refundable tax credits such as the Earned Income Tax Credit) averaged about 2.1 percent of GDP over the past four decades (see chart). These expenditures are on track to fall below that level in coming years.

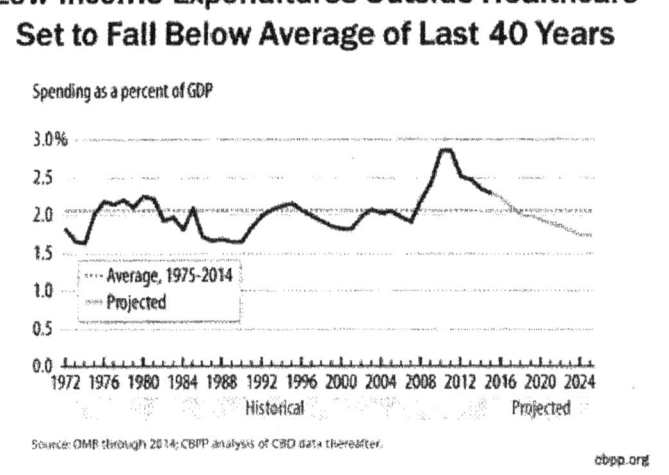

Center on Budget and Policy Priorities

**Low-Income Expenditures Outside Healthcare
Set to Fall Below Average of Last 40 Years**

Spending as a percent of GDP

Source: OMB through 2014; CBPP analysis of CBO data thereafter.

cbpp.org

4. Long-Run Fiscal Sustainability Does Not Require Balanced Budgets

The budget does not have to be balanced to reduce the economic burden of the debt. Increases in the dollar amount of debt are not a serious concern as long as the economy is growing at least as fast. For example, as the earlier chart shows, even though there were deficits in almost every year between World War II and the early 1970s, debt grew much more slowly than the economy, so the debt-to-GDP ratio fell dramatically.

Now, however, CBO projects that without policy changes, deficits and debt will rise as a share of GDP. Generally, the debt-to-GDP ratio should rise only during hard times or major emergencies and then decline during good times. That enables the government to combat recessions through temporary tax cuts and spending increases and to alleviate hardship during bad times, while creating a presumption against policies that markedly increase the debt during good times.

A stable debt-to-GDP ratio rather than a balanced budget is a key test of fiscal sustainability. Some suggest that certain debt-to-GDP ratios have a particular meaning in terms of their effect on the economy. In reality, there are no absolute thresholds.

Until a few years ago, for instance, many pointed to a 2010 analysis by economists Carmen Reinhart and Kenneth Rogoff suggesting that debt-to-GDP ratios of 90 percent or more are associated with significantly slower economic growth. But the authors have acknowledged computational errors in their original work and clarified that there is no "magic threshold" for the debt ratio above which countries suddenly pay a marked penalty in terms of slower economic growth. To the extent that countries with higher levels of debt experience slower growth, there is not much evidence that the high debt caused the slow growth; the reverse is just as likely to be true — that the slow growth caused the high debt — or some combination of the two effects.

Similarly, some analysts call for a debt ratio of 60 percent of GDP or less, a goal that the European Union and the International Monetary Fund (IMF) adopted in the 1990s. No economic evidence supports this or any other specific target, however, and IMF staff have made clear that the 60 percent criterion is arbitrary and should not guide near-term fiscal policy in the wake of the recent financial crisis, which drove up government debt worldwide. The IMF recently stated, "Our results do not identify any clear debt threshold above which medium-term growth prospects are dramatically compromised."

All else being equal, a lower debt-to-GDP ratio is preferred because of the additional flexibility it provides policymakers facing economic or financial crises and the lower interest burden it carries. But all else is never equal. Lowering the debt ratio comes at a cost, requiring larger spending cuts, higher revenues, or both. That is why it is important to look at not only the quantity but also the quality of deficit reduction, which should not hinder the economic recovery, cut spending in areas that can boost future productivity, or harm vulnerable members of society.

The Debt Limit Plays No Constructive Role in Budget Policy

Policymakers who want to improve the country's economic and budget outlook should scrap the debt limit (also known as the debt ceiling), which plays no constructive role in enforcing budget discipline. Rather, it encourages reckless brinkmanship that makes it harder to work out the compromises necessary to achieve a sustainable deficit-reduction agreement.

As CBO explains in a 2010 report:[6]

By itself, setting a limit on the debt is an ineffective means of controlling deficits because the decisions that necessitate borrowing are made through other legislative actions. By the time an increase in the debt ceiling comes up for approval, it is too late to avoid paying the government's pending bills without incurring serious negative consequences.

CBO does go on to say, "However, because increases in the debt limit have been essential, the process of considering such increases tends to bring debt levels to the forefront of policy debate." That was in 2010. But "debt levels" were already prominent in fiscal policy debates and remain there now, as this hearing shows.

---

[6] *Federal Debt and Interest Costs*, Congressional Budget Office, December 2010, p. 23, http://www.cbo.gov/sites/default/files/cbofiles/ftpdocs/119xx/doc11999/12-14-federaldebt.pdf.

1. Debt Subject to Statutory Limit Has No Economic or Financial Significance

Table 1-3 in CBO's report shows projections for several measures of federal debt. Its featured measure is debt held by the public — basically, the sum of all past deficits minus surpluses. This measure tells us what the federal government owes to outside lenders such as corporations, households, and other governments here and abroad. Changes in government borrowing from the public are significant because they can affect national saving and credit markets.

The debt limit applies to a different measure. In addition to debt held by the public, debt subject to limit includes money that the federal government owes to itself — such as the money the Social Security and Medicare trust funds have lent to the Treasury in years when their revenues exceeded their spending for benefits and other costs. Debt subject to limit is a close cousin of "gross debt" (the debt shown in those scary debt clocks). These are seriously flawed and analytically meaningless measures of the debt.

Between 1998 and 2001, for example, debt subject to limit continued to grow — even though the country was running budget *surpluses* and *retiring* some of the debt held by the public — because the Social Security trust fund was running large surpluses and lending them to the Treasury. Likewise, a policy aimed at improving long-term fiscal stability by shoring up the Social Security trust funds would reduce the deficit without reducing the debt subject to limit or the gross debt.

2. The Debt Limit Is Harmful

A recent report by the Government Accountability Office (GAO)[7] reinforces the conclusion that we would be better off without a debt limit.[8]

GAO found that in October 2013, when the Treasury was close to breaching the debt limit, "investors reported taking the unprecedented action of systematically avoiding certain Treasury securities." That cost the Treasury "from roughly $38 million to more than $70 million" in higher interest costs — amounting to, in essence, nothing more than a waste of taxpayers' money.

GAO also interviewed budget and policy experts (including some of us at CBPP) and identified three alternative ways to handle the debt limit if we were not willing to scrap it:

- Let the debt limit rise automatically or at a minimum, force an immediate vote on a "clean" debt limit increase — that is, one that's not attached to any other legislative proposals — whenever Congress adopts a new budget resolution. Congress could no longer pass a budget plan but not set a debt limit consistent with it.

- Allow the President to raise the debt limit as needed to cover bills incurred under existing budget law, while giving Congress a special, fast-track procedure to pass a law disapproving any such action.

[7] "Debt Limit: Market Responses to Recent Impasses Underscores Need to Consider Alternative Approaches," GAO-15-476, U.S. Government Accountability Office, July 9, 2015, http://www.gao.gov/products/GAO-15-476.

[8] Richard Kogan, "Federal Debt Limit's Harmful, Report Shows," Center on Budget and Policy Priorities, July 16, 2015, http://www.cbpp.org/blog/federal-debt-limits-harmful-report-shows.

• Allow the Treasury to borrow as needed to cover bills incurred under existing budget law.

Any of these alternatives is better than the current approach, in which Congress enacts spending and tax laws but doesn't have to permit the borrowing needed to cover the nation's resulting bills — and so raises the risks of what could be a catastrophic default.

GAO's conclusions mirror those of a distinguished and bipartisan group of top economists who overwhelmingly agreed in 2013, "Because all federal spending and taxes must be approved by both houses of Congress and the executive branch, a separate debt ceiling that has to be increased periodically creates unneeded uncertainty and can potentially lead to worse fiscal outcomes."[9]

And, as the *Financial Times* opined a few years ago, "Sane governments do not cast doubt on the pledge to honor their debts — which is why, if reason prevailed, the debt ceiling would simply be scrapped."

The 2011 debt-limit showdown was not pretty, and even though a default was averted, the economy and the budget did not escape unharmed. As Urban Institute Fellow Donald Marron, a former acting CBO director and a member of President George W. Bush's Council of Economic Advisers, testified in 2013 before the Joint Economic Committee, "brinksmanship does not come free."[10]

Through accident or miscalculation, games of chicken can sometimes end in a crash, and the costs to the United States of actually defaulting on its financial obligations could be very high. If prolonged, a situation in which the Treasury is required to match payments to available cash would have an economic effect like sequestration on steroids and would likely plunge the economy back into recession. Even if the debt limit were subsequently raised, the damage to the U.S. credit rating likely would harm us for years to come.

To my knowledge, only one other developed country, Denmark, has a statutory debt limit anything like ours. Both countries have put a dollar limit on how much debt the government can issue. There's a crucial difference, however, between our debt limit and Denmark's: the Danes do not play politics with theirs, as Jacob Funk Kirkegaard of the Peterson Institute for International Economics explains:[11]

The Danish fixed nominal debt limit — legislatively outside the annual budget process — was created solely in response to an administrative reorganization among the institutions of government in Denmark and the requirements of the Danish Constitution. It was never intended to play any role in day-to-day politics.

---

[9] "Debt Ceiling," IGM Forum, January 15, 2013, http://www.igmchicago.org/igm-economic-experts-panel/poll-results?SurveyID=SV_555sdN4BXmfNKCN.

[10] Donald Marron, "The Costs of Debt Limit Brinksmanship," Tax Policy Center, September 18, 2013, http://www.taxpolicycenter.org/publications/url.cfm?ID=904601.

[11] Jacob Funk Kirkegaard, "Can a Debt Ceiling Be Sensible? The Case of Denmark II," Peterson Institute for International Economics, July 28, 2011, http://www.piie.com/blogs/realtime/?p=2292.

When the financial crisis caused a sharp increase in government debt in 2008-2009, the Danes raised their debt ceiling — a lot. The 2010 increase doubled the existing ceiling, which was already well above the actual debt, to nearly three times the debt at the time. As Kirkegaard reports, "The explicit intent of this move — supported incidentally by all the major parties in the Danish parliament — was to ensure that the Danish debt ceiling remained far in excess of outstanding debt and would never play a role in day-to-day politics."

The Constitution gives Congress power over federal borrowing, which it has exercised for decades through the statutory limit on federal debt. But the government is also legally bound to honor its financial obligations. Holding the debt limit hostage risks provoking a governance crisis in which the President is forced to choose between breaking the law by ignoring the debt ceiling or breaking the law by not paying government obligations in a timely manner. In terms of limiting economic damage, the former is by far the better choice.

3. Debt Prioritization Proposal Is Extremely Dangerous

Legislation like H.R. 692 that would allow Treasury to borrow funds to pay bondholders and Social Security recipients if there's a prolonged standoff over raising the debt ceiling is extremely dangerous. By appearing to make a default legitimate and manageable, it would heighten the risk that one will actually occur.

Millions of people beyond bondholders and Social Security beneficiaries depend on timely federal payments. H.R. 692 says nothing about how the Treasury can pay veterans, troops, doctors and hospitals that treat Medicare patients, state and local governments, private contractors, and recipients of unemployment insurance, SNAP, and Supplemental Security Income.

The Treasury makes roughly 80 million separate payments each month, so deciding which bills to pay would be extremely difficult, even if interest and Social Security benefits could be pulled out and paid. And domestic and foreign lenders would hardly be reassured at the sight of Treasury grappling with how to meet its legal obligations when cash is short.

During a standoff over raising the debt ceiling in early 2013, one rating agency explicitly warned that honoring interest and principal payments but delaying payment on other obligations would trigger a review and possible downgrade of the nation's creditworthiness. At that time, the Economist called failing to raise the debt limit and attempting to prioritize payments an "instrument of mass financial destruction."

Conclusion

I respectfully disagree with the view that unsustainable federal spending is the sole force driving projected future deficits and debt, that balancing the budget is necessary to achieve fiscal sustainability, or that the debt ceiling has any constructive role to play in budget policy.

New revenues will have to be a part of any realistic effort to achieve fiscal sustainability and meet 21st century national needs. Policymakers will have to be willing to buckle down and make compromises. Revenues were a part of every major deficit reduction package in the 1980s and 1990s until the Balanced Budget Act of 1997.[12]

Holding budget negotiations hostage to the debt limit and trying to pretend that it is legitimate and manageable to do so is a new and dangerous tactic. Congress should take away that temptation by following one of the GAO's recommendations or, better yet, scrapping the debt limit altogether.

---

[12] Kathy Ruffing, "The Composition of Past Deficit-Reduction Packages – And Lessons for the Next One," Center on Budget and Policy Priorities, November 15, 2011, http://www.cbpp.org/research/the-composition-of-past-deficit-reduction-packages-and-lessons-for-the-next-one?fa=view&id=3617.

www.ingramcontent.com/pod-product-compliance
Lightning Source LLC
Chambersburg PA
CBHW081235280526
45787CB00006B/2667